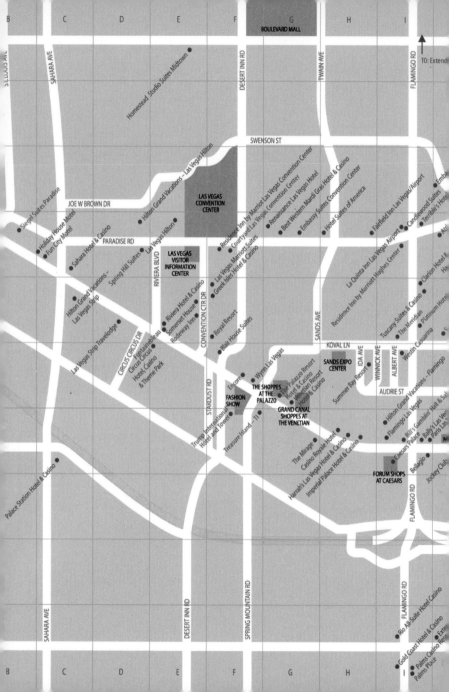

# LAS VEGAS
## COCKTAILS

### AN ELEGANT COLLECTION OF OVER 100 RECIPES INSPIRED BY SIN CITY

### SIVAN GAVISH

CIDER MILL PRESS

BOOK PUBLISHERS

# LAS VEGAS COCKTAILS

13-Digit ISBN: 978-1-60433-957-4
10-Digit ISBN: 1-60433-957-8

This book may be ordered by mail from the publisher. Please include $5.99 for postage and handling. Please support your local bookseller first!

Books published by Cider Mill Press Book Publishers are available at special discounts for bulk purchases in the United States by corporations, institutions, and other organizations. For more information, please contact the publisher.

Cider Mill Press Book Publishers
"Where good books are ready for press"
PO Box 454
12 Spring Street
Kennebunkport, Maine 04046
Visit us online!
cidermillpress.com

Photo Credits: Pages 4-5: Carol M. Highsmith, "Jackpot! Las Vegas, Nevada," ca. 1980-2006, courtesy Library of Congress; page 7: Arthur Rothstein, "Main Street. Las Vegas, Nevada," 1940, courtesy Library of Congress; pages 8-9: West Coast Art Co., "Las Vegas, Nevada," ca. 1910, courtesy Library of Congress; pages 22 and 25: courtesy 1923 Bourbon Bar; page 26: courtesy Barbershop; pages 28, 31-32, 36, 39, 40, 42, 45-46, 64-65, 76, 79, 96-99, 101, 140, 143-144, 146, 149, 153, 164, 170-171, 174, 178, 184, 186, 194, 197-198, 202, 205-206, 212, 216, 222, 225-226, 228, 230, 232, 235-236, 244, 256, 259-260, 262, 264, 272-273, 275-276, 279-282, and 285: Sivan Gavish; pages 34-35: Rick Morrison Photography, courtesy Breeze Daiquiri Bar; pages 52, 55-56, 154, and 157-158: 50 Eggs Hospitality Group; pages 60, 62 and 114: Mister Brittany, Inc. (Samuel Ross, President); pages 106, 109, and 112: Jeff Green Photography, courtesy Mr. COCO; pages 164 and 167-168: Bryan Hainer, courtesy Timeless Cuisine; pages 188, 191-192: Studio West Photography, courtesy Frankie's Tiki Room; page 218: Cheyenne Lane, courtesy No Regrets; pages 238 and 241: Sabin Orr Photography, courtesy Sparrow + Wolf; pages 266 and 269-270: Ian Maltzman courtesy of Downtown Cocktail Room; pages 286 and 289-290: Ian Maltzman courtesy Mike Morey's; pages 292 and 295: courtesy Oak & Ivy; pages 310 and 313: Bianca Scott, courtesy of Velveteen Rabbit.

All other images used under official license from Shutterstock.com.

Typography: Avenir, Copperplate, Nobel, Sackers, Warnock

Printed in China

1 2 3 4 5 6 7 8 9 0

First Edition

# CONTENTS

VIVA LAS VEGAS! • 5

THE STRIP • 19

OFF THE STRIP • 161

DOWNTOWN • 249

INDEX • 316

# VIVA LAS VEGAS!

**W**elcome to Las Vegas—the city that never sleeps. Wait, that's accurate, but is more commonly applied to New York. Sin City. Yup, that sounds right. There are so many names we can give Las Vegas, but for now let's stick with Sin City. To be clear, it's not all about sin here. Sure, it's built upon, and known for, gambling, drinking, and dancing. However, this exquisite city is also full of opportunities, glamor, magic, and beauty. In addition to those attributes, Las Vegas embraces diversity like few other towns.

Any Vegas resident will tell you: wherever we go in the world, it's the same set of responses when we share that we call Las Vegas home. The usual reply is "No way, what's it like?" "Viva Las Vegas!" is another popular one. People go nuts for this town, and with good reason. As a local, I understand this reaction and quite honestly, I welcome it. The fact that people from all over the world know Las Vegas and save thousands of dollars just to travel here helps me appreciate how lucky I've been to land here. It truly is a special place, and I feel so blessed to call it home.

Las Vegans share a camaraderie that many people from out of town don't realize. People here are kind, friendly, and ready to work as a team. I've always said it, and I stand by it. We fight for each other and we lift each other up. Spend a weekend here, on and off The Strip, and you'll see what I'm talking about. It takes multitudes to keep this city humming, and those of us who live and work here know that no

matter our profession, we are part of what draws millions of visitors to our desert oasis year after year.

Some of the top chefs and mixologists came to Las Vegas with the same thoughts and feelings anyone hitting the city for a long weekend might carry in, but they stayed and created a world-class dining scene that everyone knows and loves. Not only because they love this city, but because of the people and the relationships that can be created here. What better way to highlight their stories and share their drinks than *Las Vegas Cocktails*?

Las Vegas was named by Rafael Rivera, a Spanish Explorer, in 1829 while traveling from New Mexico to Los Angeles. Rivera made a stop on the Old Spanish Road during his journey and discovered artesian wells surrounded by green land. He tabbed the valley "Las Vegas," which in Spanish means "The Meadows."

In 1905, after the completion of a railroad line that connected Los Angeles to Salt Lake City and passed through the town, Las Vegas was officially founded. Farmers were first attracted to the area in the early 1900s, but the real boom began when ground was broken on Boulder Dam in 1930, which created the 115-mile-long Lake Mead, one of the world's largest artificial lakes. The dam was

renamed Hoover Dam in 1931, to honor the president under whose administration construction began, though that appellation didn't truly stick until President Truman signed a bill formalizing the name in 1947. By 1931, the Las Vegas population had grown to around 25,000 citizens. No matter what it was called, the huge project attracted many workers to the area and laid the groundwork for urban infrastructure by virtue of hydroelectricity, irrigation, and a domestic water supply. Las Vegas as we know it today grew out of the Hoover Dam.

Since the demographics at the time consisted of mostly male workers, the entertainment market developed. Showgirl theaters became increasingly popular, along with a few licensed casinos on Fremont Street (the first paved street in Las Vegas). So began the rise of the gaming capital of the world.

The "Sin City" nickname took hold after local entrepreneurs in an area known as "Block 16" began renting out the backrooms of their bars to prostitutes, who would give the associated establishment a cut of their earnings. While prostitution is legal in some parts of Nevada, it is now illegal in Las Vegas. The reputation for "sin" was also bolstered by the role organized crime played in starting many of the casinos on The Strip, which helped Las Vegas grow from an Old Spanish Road town to a global destination.

Fast-forward to today and Las Vegas has become one of the fastest growing cities in America. It is also consistently ranked as one of the world's most popular tourist destinations.

That rapid growth has brought a lot of changes with it. There was the unthinkable horror and tragedy of the mass shooting that occurred on October 1, 2017. There was also the arrival of sports venues like the T-Mobile Arena, home to the National Hockey League's Golden Knights, and the Las Vegas Ballpark, home of the Aviators, a minor league baseball team. Both venues helped rebuild the city's spirit after the tragedy struck.

With all that's been going on, I was worried that I would not be able to give this city the tribute that it deserves in this book. The pressure was large and I hope that you, the reader, feel as much love reading this as I felt while writing and researching.

I grew up here, and I thought I knew everything I needed to know. Boy, was I wrong. Give yourself six weeks in any city to dive deep into a specific topic—booze in particular—and you will learn more than you ever thought possible.

The people I met, the connections I made, and the experiences I had throughout this journey could fill another book. Doing the research and legwork to put together this book provided many moments that will forever be near and dear to my heart. The openness of these mixologists was astounding, and the biggest thing I learned is that we all have hopes and dreams. Their craft is truly an art form, and it is an absolute honor to be able to highlight those who have dedicated their lives to perfecting it.

Everyone featured in this book has taken the time to create cocktails unique to their venues. Their stories, backgrounds, and history with Vegas have been documented throughout. If you're a local, you're

sure to find some new favorite spots; if you're visiting, I urge you to wander off The Strip (though there are plenty of excellent drinks to be had there, too). No matter where you live, the biggest piece of advice I have for you—and this was the biggest piece of advice given to me by the best bartenders in Vegas—is to branch out and try something new. At your next outing, ask for a cocktail menu and try something different. Tell the bartender what you like and ask them to surprise you with something special. At the end of the day, they are creating art in liquid form, and every artist thrives when asked to let their creativity run wild.

Don't leave the drinking until your next visit to Las Vegas. Trust me, there is not a bad drink in this book. Just taste for yourself. Create these drinks in the comfort of your own home, and imagine you're enjoying them here in Vegas. My hope is that you, too, can learn how to become a mixologist. With the recipes, tips, and tricks held within, you and your guests will be drinking like a Las Vegan in no time!

# BUILDING YOUR VEGAS BAR

There are so many different options when building a home bar. It can be built into your home, or purchased online or in a store. One slightly-off-the-beaten-path option: a bar cart. It is perfect for home bartending, providing a work space and plenty of storage. They are also very easy to tailor to your liking with your favorite spirits, mixers, glasses, accessories, and tools.

## Tools

If you're just getting into cocktails, keep it simple. Too many tools will become overwhelming and might just turn you off from cocktail making altogether. When you're starting out, the following items should put you in position to succeed. Make sure you don't skimp on these items, as you want them to last.

*Mixing Glass:* This is essentially a large glass where you'll put the ingredients to stir them. Ideally, it will have a little lip, making it easy and fast to pour from.

*Mixing/Bar Spoon:* A long, thin spoon, typically with a spiralled shaft, designed for stirring drinks. Some cocktail recipes will call for a bar spoon of certain ingredients, which is equal to 1 teaspoon.

*Shaker:* Possibly the most important tool in mixology. You'll shake your ingredients together in it to mix and chill as required. There are different types on the market but it is probably better to avoid one with a built-in strainer; those are harder to clean and tricky for handling egg whites and other ingredients.

*Strainer:* To separate certain solid bits from your liquid as you pour. A Hawthorne strainer is a great choice as it can be securely fitted over a shaker or mixing glass. A julep strainer, which has a perforated surface, is another widely available option.

*Fine Strainer:* A mesh strainer that catches smaller particles, like pulp and ice chips.

*Cheesecloth:* This is to filter your drinks and, occasionally, syrups as thoroughly as possible. A few recipes call for this, although coffee filters can also provide the desired results.

*Jiggers:* Handy little measuring utensils that ensure you get your ingredient proportions right. Make sure you get ones with the measurements you think you will need most.

*Juice Press:* Mostly for making fresh lemon and lime juice, which you will need to do often.

*Muddler:* A bartender's pestle, used to mash fruit, herbs, and spices in the bottom of a glass or shaker to help release their flavor.

*Ice Trays:* Various recipes call for different types of ice. Ideally, have trays that can do normal-sized cubes, spheres, and larger blocks. An ice crusher, for crushed ice, can be useful, too.

*Glasses:* At the very least, have some rocks glasses, but highball glasses are also useful, as are coupes and/or cocktail glasses. These will cover almost all types of cocktails and the glasses that they would require (or can replace other types of glasses with a similar profile).

## SPIRITS

Unless you'll be entertaining all week long, no need to go crazy here. Focus more on quality than quantity. A few bottles of your favorite spirits will do: gin, vodka, rum, tequila, and whiskey. Your setup will look nice with a bottle or two displayed and the rest tucked away. Ask yourself what you prefer. Dark, light, or sweet? Are you making more Negronis or Margaritas? Your answers will be a tell-tale sign for which spirits should be in your bar.

## Liqueurs and Mixers

*Orange Liqueurs:* Whether triple sec, Cointreau, or Grand Marnier, these always will be useful.

*Dry and Sweet Vermouth:* At a minimum, you want one bottle of each on hand at all times. Martini & Rossi is one of the go-to sweet vermouths and Noilly Prat is a popular dry one.

*Cherry Liqueur:* Luxardo maraschino cherry liqueur is common, but Cherry Heering is great, too.

*St-Germain:* A popular elderflower liqueur that adds unique floral notes to a drink.

*Sparkling Wine:* Sparkling cocktails are becoming more popular, so it might be useful to have a spare bottle of Champagne or sparkling wine handy.

*Bitters:* You will often use Angostura but there is a wide world of choices that provide many flavors.

*Citrus:* At the minimum, have a good amount of lemons and limes on hand so you can make fresh juice and garnishes. Don't hesitate to go for grapefruits and oranges, too, if you think you might use them.

*Simple Syrup:* Place 1 part sugar and 1 part water in a saucepan and bring to a simmer, stirring gently until the sugar dissolves. Let the mix cool before bottling and storing in the fridge for up to 1 month.

*Rich Simple Syrup:* The same process as above, only it uses 2 parts sugar to 1 part water. It will last up to 6 months in the fridge.

*Juices:* Apple, tomato, pineapple, cranberry—anything you like the taste of really.

*Carbonated Mixers:* Quality tonic water, because Gin & Tonics are always called for. But if you have the space, soda water, ginger ale, and cola are good to have on hand.

*Herbs:* Basil and mint are great for garnishes and easy infusions. Rosemary and thyme can also add some great flavors. Feel free to experiment with any others you might like.

## Techniques and Terms in Recipes

*Shake:* If the recipe calls for the cocktail to be shaken (and many in this book do), make sure you fill your shaker about halfway with ice cubes (unless instructed otherwise) before adding your ingredients. Shake vigorously for 10 to 20 seconds.

*Dry Shake:* A dry shake means that you shake the ingredients without adding any ice to the cocktail shaker. This will help viscous ingredients like egg whites emulsify.

*Strain:* Ensures that the ice (or other chunky things) from a shaker or mixing glass do not get into your glass.

*Double-Strain:* Pouring the contents of the cocktail shaker through a fine strainer or a mesh strainer in addition to the strainer that will remove the chunky elements.

*Stir:* Another common mixing method. Fill a mixing glass with ice and pour in the required ingredients. Using a bar spoon, find its balance point (usually around two-thirds up the spoon), and use a pushing-and-pulling motion while rotating the wrist to ensure that the ingredients are mixed together without agitation. It takes a little practice to do well, but once you get it, it's a useful skill.

*Mist:* Simply put the liquid that needs to be misted into a spray bottle or use an atomizer top in order to gently spray the mist around the glass or on top of the drink.

### Accessories

Colorful straws, coasters, cocktail umbrellas (for your Margaritas and Piña Coladas, of course), napkins, cocktail picks, carafes, and ice buckets are highly recommended. As is having fun. As is keeping a copy of *Las Vegas Cocktails* close by.

# THE STRIP

BARREL-AGED OLD FASHIONED • GATSBY'S GIN FIZZ • MUSTACHE RIDE • BOUND OLD FASHIONED • THE RESTED ROOT • SPICY FIFTY • BREEZE DAQUIRI • CAKE BOSS • DRAGO ROSO • MARGARITA VENEZIANA • ESPRESSO MARTINI • RASPBERRY LEMON DROP • SOMETHING DELICIOUS • VIDEO KILLED THE RADIO STAR • VERBENA • SOME LIKE IT HOT • F. W. MARGARITA • FLOR DE LA PIÑA • GET HIM TO THE GREEK • COCONUT WHITE RUSSIAN • DISGRUNTLED MAI TAI • FAT TUESDAY DAQUIRI • THE MAVERICK • COSMOPOLITAN FLIGHT • MEZCAL SUN • MOLE NEGRONI • G • THE DESTROYER • DOPE HAT • ROOK • FAT CAP • QUEEN'S PARK SWIZZLE • BARREL-AGED TONY NEGRONI • MILANO • NIGHT AT THE OPERA • ITALIAN HIGHBALL • ACQUA DI VIDA • FROSTED BERRIES • NORTHERN LIGHTS • MR. COCO • THE VICKY • NEGRONI BIANCO • BANCO DE MEXICO • SARU 47 • OLD SMOKEY KNIGHTS • WALK THIS WAY • UTOPIA • BUOL MULE • LEVEL 55: GHOSTBAR • STRAWBERRY COBBLER • CUCUMBER STILETTO • SPICE OF LOVE • RUM 'N' BRAMBLE • ATOMIC FIZZ • SCRATCH MARGARITA • BEHOLD THE GOLD • OWEN'S MEGA MULE • PINK JASMINE MARTINI • OWEN'S SPRITZ • NOLET US PRAY • IL GEORGIO • PARADISO • BLACKBERRY BOURBON LEMONADE • SOUTHERN REVIVAL • YARDBIRD OLD FASHIONED

Lined with resort hotels and casinos, The Strip is what most people think of when they think of Las Vegas. Considering that, it's interesting that this 4.2-mile-long stretch of road is actually south of the official city limits. Then again, it is often the only place that people visit, and the city gets a lot of visitors, over 42 million between 2000 and 2018.

# 1923 BOURBON BAR

The entrance to this hidden gem is underneath a set of escalators in Mandalay Bay.

# – BARREL-AGED OLD FASHIONED –

A twist on a traditional Old Fashioned, which makes sense for a bar styled after a Prohibition-era speakeasy. Back then, booze was a black-market purchase and speakeasies had to make do with what was available locally, a concession they frequently masked by using those liquors in cocktails. Luckily, the bourbon used here—which is distilled by the small-batch specialists at Nevada H & C Distilling Co.—is award-winning.

GLASSWARE: **Rocks glass**

GARNISH: **Strip of orange peel**

- **1½ oz. Smoke Wagon Bourbon**
- **½ oz. Pierre Ferrand Dry Curaçao**
- **½ oz. Amaro Nonino**
- **1 dash cherry bitters**

1. Build the cocktail in rocks glass filled with ice and gently stir until chilled.

2. Garnish with the strip of orange peel.

# – GATSBY'S GIN FIZZ –

N o throwback to the Roaring Twenties would be complete without a reference to *The Great Gatsby*, and this cocktail would fit
right in at one of Jay's famously riotous gatherings.

GLASSWARE: **Coupe**

GARNISH: **Strip of lemon peel**

- 1½ oz. Tanqueray gin
- ½ oz. Simple Syrup (see page 15)
- 1 oz. sour mix (see page 177 for homemade)
- ½ oz. egg white
- 1 splash club soda
- 1 squeeze fresh lemon juice
- 1 dash Angostura Bitters

1. Add all of the ingredients to a cocktail shaker filled with ice, shake vigorously until chilled, and strain into the coupe.

2. Garnish with the strip of lemon peel.

BARBERSHOP

# – MUSTACHE RIDE –

The speakeasy theme is done so well at this Cosmopolitan Hotel spot that if you didn't know there was a bar hidden behind an actual barbershop you'd never venture in—unless you needed a haircut.

GLASSWARE: **Coupe**

GARNISH: **Black Islay Mustache**

- 1½ oz. Writers' Tears Copper Pot Irish Whiskey
- 1 oz. Cherry Heering
- ¾ oz. Vanilla Orgeat
- 2 oz. Guinness Draught
- 1 dash black Islay bitters

1. Add all of the ingredients to a cocktail shaker filled with ice, shake vigorously until chilled, and strain into the coupe.

2. Garnish by drawing the Black Islay Mustache on top of the cocktail.

VANILLA ORGEAT: Preheat the oven to 400°F. Place 2 cups almonds on a baking sheet and toast in the oven for 5 minutes. Remove and let cool. Once cool, pulverize the nuts in a food processor, blender, or grain mill. Add the almond meal to a standard Simple Syrup (see page 15) after the sugar has dissolved. Remove the pan from heat and let the mixture stand for 3 to 6 hours. Strain the mixture through cheesecloth and discard the solids. Add 1 teaspoon rose water, 2 oz. vodka, and 3 tablespoons pure vanilla extract, stir to incorporate, and store in the refrigerator for up to 3 weeks.

BLACK ISLAY MUSTACHE: In a small bowl, stir activated charcoal powder and Laphroaig 10-Year-Old Scotch together to create a thick liquid. Using a dropper, draw up the mixture. Drop 6 dots of the mixture on the cocktail's froth and then use a toothpick to connect them and form the "mustache."

# – BOUND OLD FASHIONED –

The ice spheres contained within the Bound Old Fashioned have the bar's logo engraved into them.

GLASSWARE: **Rocks glass**

GARNISH: **Orange twist and brandied cherry**

- 1 sugar cube
- 5 dashes Angostura Bitters
- 1 splash water
- 2 oz. Woodford Reserve bourbon

1. Place the sugar cube in a mixing glass, add the bitters and water, and muddle.

2. Add ice and then slowly add the bourbon while stirring the cocktail.

3. Strain over a large ice sphere into a rocks glass and garnish with the orange twist and brandied cherry.

# – THE RESTED ROOT –

**D**ominick DeMartino won the Herradura Legends competition with this drink, beating out 3,000 entries and 12 selected competitors.

**GLASSWARE:** Cocktail glass

**GARNISH:** Dehydrated orange wheel (see page 166) and fresh mint leaf

- 2 oz. Herradura Reposado Tequila
- 1 oz. fresh lemon juice
- ½ oz. Domaine de Canton
- ½ oz. Velvet Falernum
- ½ oz. Ginger Reàl
- 5 dashes Angostura Bitters

1. Add all of the ingredients to a cocktail shaker filled with ice, shake vigorously until chilled, and strain into the cocktail glass.

2. Garnish with a dehydrated orange wheel and a mint leaf.

# — SPICY FIFTY —

Do not let the name nor the chili pepper garnish fool you, as this isn't a terribly spicy cocktail. In fact, the vanilla vodka and syrups give it a subtle sweetness. If you do like heat, simply add more pepper slices to the shaker.

GLASSWARE: **Cocktail glass**

GARNISH: **Red chili pepper**

- 1 ¾ oz. Stoli Vanil vodka
- ½ oz. Elderflower Syrup
- ½ oz. fresh lime juice
- ¼ oz. Honey Syrup (see page 185)
- 2 thin slices chili pepper

1. Add all of the ingredients to a cocktail shaker filled with ice, shake vigorously until chilled, and strain into the cocktail glass.

2. Garnish with red chili pepper perched on rim.

ELDERFLOWER SYRUP: Place 1 cup water, 1 cup sugar, and 2 tablespoons lemon juice in a saucepan and bring to a simmer, stirring until the sugar has dissolved. Remove the pan from heat, add the flowers from 5 freshly picked elderflower clusters to the syrup, and steep for 3 to 5 days. Strain before using or storing.

## BREEZE DAIQUIRI BAR

Slush bars, also known as Daquiri bars, are ubiquitous on The Strip. With open containers permitted outdoors in this part of town, many tourists gravitate toward these drinks as they wander around, and for good reason: they don't taste like alcohol and they last a long time— just look at the size of these things. Since Breeze Daquiri's drinks are batched and made in large machines, there is not an exact recipe. But these flavors can provide direction for a beverage that can be created at home and tailored to your preferences. Breeze Daiquiri Bar offers: strawberry colada, mango, piña colada, strawberry, green apple, and sour apple.

BUDDY V'S

# – CAKE BOSS –

**B**uddy Valastro, star of *Cake Boss*, says: "No matter what the recipe, any baker can do wonders in the kitchen with some good ingredients and an upbeat attitude!" So true, and the ingredients in this drink make it look and taste like a decadent chocolate cake.

GLASSWARE: **Cocktail glass**

GARNISH: **Cake crumbs**

- **2 oz. Pinnacle Cake Vodka**
- **1 oz. Marie Brizard Royal Chocolat**
- **Baileys Irish Cream, to top**

1. Add the vodka and chocolate liqueur to a cocktail shaker filled with ice, shake vigorously until chilled, and strain into chilled cocktail glass.

2. Pour the Baileys over the back of a spoon to float it on top of the cocktail and garnish with the cake crumbs.

# – DRAGO ROSO –

PAMA Pomegranate Flavored Liqueur and pomegranate molasses are the standouts in this cocktail. Both smell like pomegranate, but the pomegranate molasses has more of the fruity, tart notes pomegranate is famed for. Sweetness from the pineapple juice and spice from the serrano pepper add those extra dimensions that are required to make a cocktail memorable.

**GLASSWARE:** **Highball glass**
**GARNISH:** **Strip of candied mango and slice of serrano pepper**

- 1 serrano pepper, or to taste, chopped
- 1¾ oz. Absolut Juice vodka
- 1 oz. mango juice
- ½ oz. PAMA Pomegranate Flavored Liqueur
- ½ oz. pineapple juice
- ¾ oz. pomegranate molasses

1. Add the serrano pepper to a cocktail shaker and muddle.

2. Add ice and the remaining ingredients, shake vigorously until chilled, and strain into the highball glass.

3. Garnish with a strip of candied mango and a slice of serrano pepper.

# — MARGARITA VENEZIANA —

This fresh, full-bodied take on a traditional Margarita pays homage to the opulent Venetian, home to Buddy V's.

GLASSWARE: **Highball glass**

GARNISH: **Lime wedge and Fabbri Amarena Cherry**

- Salt, for the rim
- 2 oz. Casamigos Blanco Tequila
- 1 oz. amaretto
- 1 oz. sour mix (see page 177 for homemade)
- ½ oz. fresh lime juice
- ½ oz. orange juice
- ¾ oz. Fabbri Amarena Cherry syrup

1. Wet the rim of a highball glass and dip the rim into the salt.

2. Add all of the remaining ingredients to a cocktail shaker filled with ice, shake vigorously until chilled, and strain into the highball glass.

3. Garnish with a lime wedge and a Fabbri Amarena Cherry.

CAFÉ AMERICANO

# – ESPRESSO MARTINI –

Located inside Caesar's Palace, Café Americano is open 24 hours a day, 365 days a year. That means you can imbibe this boozy pick-me-up morning, noon, or night.

GLASSWARE: **Cocktail glass**

GARNISH: **3 espresso beans**

- • **1 oz. brewed espresso**
- • **2½ oz. Three Olives Vanilla Vodka**
- • **½ oz. Kahlùa**
- • **¼ oz. crème de cacao**

1. Chill the cocktail glass.

2. Add all of the ingredients to a cocktail shaker filled with ice, shake vigorously until chilled, and strain into the chilled glass.

3. Garnish with the espresso beans, placing them all in a row.

# – RASPBERRY LEMON DROP –

G et that long weekend started with this overwhelmingly tasty Martini variation.

**GLASSWARE:** Cocktail glass

**GARNISH:** None

- Sugar, for the rim
- 4 blueberries
- 2 oz. Three Olives Raspberry Vodka
- ¼ oz. triple sec
- 1 splash cranberry juice
- 1 squeeze fresh lemon juice
- ½ oz. Chambord, for bottom of glass

1. Wet the rim of the cocktail glass and dip it into the sugar.

2. Place the blueberries in a cocktail shaker and muddle.

3. Add the vodka, triple sec, and juices to the shaker along with ice. Shake vigorously until chilled and then strain into the cocktail glass.

4. Pour the Chambord over the back of a spoon, allowing it to settle into a layer at the bottom of the glass.

# – SOMETHING DELICIOUS –

**D**o you want to try something delicious? Yes. Yes, you do.

GLASSWARE: **Mason jar**

GARNISH: **Lime wheel**

- 1½ oz. Three Olives Raspberry Vodka
- ¼ oz. triple sec
- ¼ oz. St-Germain
- ¼ oz. sweet & sour mix (see page 190 for homemade)
- 1 splash cranberry juice

1. Add all of the ingredients to a cocktail shaker filled with ice, shake vigorously until chilled, and strain over ice into a mason jar.

2. Garnish with the lime wheel.

THE CHANDELIER AT
COSMOPOLITAN

# – VIDEO KILLED THE RADIO STAR –

The coconut foam is made with coconut milk, black pepper, and carda-mom, and it goes wonderfully with the slightly grassy taste of caçhaca.

GLASSWARE: **Coupe**

GARNISH: **Edible rice paper with "Pop" or "Bang" printed on it**

- **1 oz. Prata Avuá Caçhaca**
- **½ oz. Giffard Crème de Fruits de la Passion**
- **½ oz. Italicus Rosolio di Bergamotto**
- **1 oz. fresh lemon juice**
- **¾ oz. apricot puree**
- **½ oz. Spiced Honey Syrup**
- **Spiced Coconut Foam, to top**

1. Add all of the ingredients, except for the Spiced Coconut Foam, to a cocktail shaker filled with ice, shake vigorously until chilled, and strain into the coupe.

2. Top with the Spiced Coconut Foam and garnish with the edible rice paper.

SPICED HONEY SYRUP: In a saucepan, combine 1 liter honey, 1 liter water, ¼ cup black peppercorns, 2 cups crushed green cardamom pods, and 6 cinnamon sticks and bring to a boil. Turn the heat to low and simmer for 20 minutes. Remove the pan from heat, let cool, and strain before using or storing.

SPICED COCONUT FOAM: Place 1 liter Spiced Honey Syrup, 1 liter Coconut Cream, and 1 liter pasteurized egg whites into iSi container, double-charge with nitrous oxide, and refrigerate.

COCONUT CREAM: Blend 1 liter half-and-half with 1½ liters Coco Lopez Cream of Coconut and keep refrigerated

# – VERBENA –

This Asian-inflected Margarita is a very popular drink at the Chandelier. The buzz button, or Szechuan flower, contains a natural alkaloid that stimulates your salivary glands and turns you into something of a super taster. As you sip your Margarita, you will become acquainted with a far more nuanced drink than the one you know.

GLASSWARE: **Rocks glass**

GARNISH: **Lemon wheel and buzz button**

- 1½ oz. Herradura Blanco Tequila
- 1 oz. Ginger Syrup
- 1 oz. fresh lemon juice

- 2 oz. Sour Mix (see page 177, substitute yuzu juice for the lime juice)

1. Add all of the ingredients to a cocktail shaker filled with ice, shake vigorously until chilled, and strain over crushed ice into a rocks glass.

2. Garnish with the buzz button.

GINGER SYRUP: Place equal parts ginger juice and sugar in a saucepan and warm over medium heat, while stirring, until the sugar has dissolved. Remove from heat and let cool before using or storing.

CHICA

# – SOME LIKE IT HOT –

**D**os Armadillos Resposado is a rested tequila with notes of vanilla, pepper, and spice.

GLASSWARE: **Blue goblet**

GARNISH: **None**

- 1 teaspoon papaya sugar, for the rim
- 1 teaspoon salt
- 1 teaspoon lime zest
- ¾ oz. fresh lime juice

- 1½ oz. Dos Armadillos Reposado Tequila
- ¾ oz. Simple Syrup (see page 15)
- ½ oz. Papaya Jam

1. Place the papaya sugar, salt, and lime zest on a small dish and stir to combine. Wet the rim of the goblet and dip it into the mixture. Fill the goblet with crushed ice.

2. Add the remaining ingredients to a cocktail shaker filled with ice, shake vigorously until chilled, and strain into the goblet.

PAPAYA JAM (YIELDS 4 QUARTS): Skin 6 papayas, cut each one in half, remove the seeds, and cut into chunks. Halve 8 habanero peppers. Place the papayas and peppers in a large saucepan with 2 quarts orange juice and 8 oz. sugar, bring to a boil, and then simmer for 30 minutes. Let cool, puree in a blender, and store in the refrigerator for up to 3 weeks.

# – F. W. MARGARITA –

The watermelon juice provides this cocktail the sweetness it deserves.

GLASSWARE: **Rocks glass**
GARNISH: **Fresh cilantro leaf and strip of lemon peel**

- 1½ oz. Espolón Tequila
- ¾ oz. fresh lime juice
- ½ oz. Fresno Chili Syrup
- 1 oz. watermelon juice
- 3 fresh cilantro leaves
- 1 dash orange bitters

1. Add all of the ingredients to a cocktail shaker filled with ice, shake vigorously until chilled, and double-strain over ice into a rocks glass.

2. Garnish with an additional cilantro leaf and a strip of lemon peel.

FRESNO CHILI SYRUP: Remove stems from 6 Fresno chili peppers and add to a food processor along with 4 quarts Simple Syrup (see page 15). Blitz until smooth and strain before using or storing.

# – FLOR DE LA PIÑA –

**A** fruity cocktail with a spicy kick. The Hibiscus & Habanero Syrup is a quick and easy way to incorporate brilliant color and additional punch.

GLASSWARE: **Rocks glass**

GARNISH: **Hibiscus flower and fresh sage leaf**

- 1½ oz. Espolón Tequila
- ¾ oz. fresh lime juice
- ½ oz. Hibiscus & Habanero Syrup
- 1 oz. pineapple juice
- 3 fresh sage leaves
- 1 dash orange bitters

1. Add all of the ingredients to a cocktail shaker filled with ice, shake vigorously until chilled, and strain over ice into a rocks glass.

2. Garnish with a hibiscus flower and an additional sage leaf.

HIBISCUS & HABANERO SYRUP (YIELDS 4 QUARTS): Halve 3 habanero peppers. In a large saucepan, combine peppers with ½ lb. dried hibiscus blossoms, 2 quarts sugar, and 4 quarts water and bring to a boil. Once boiling, lower heat and simmer for 30 minutes. Strain before using or storing.

CLIQUE

# – GET HIM TO THE GREEK –

Yogurt is far from a conventional addition to a cocktail, but the creamy texture and tangy flavor it supplies, when accompanied by the dill, work very well with the gin in this drink. Don't be surprised if you start seeing yogurt popping up on more bar menus.

GLASSWARE: **Coupe**

GARNISH: **Cucumber slice and sprig of fresh dill**

- 1½ oz. Bulldog Gin
- 1 oz. plain yogurt
- 1¼ oz. fresh lemon juice
- 1 sprig of fresh dill
- 2 tablespoons chopped cucumber

1. Add all of the ingredients to a cocktail shaker filled with ice, shake vigorously until chilled, and strain over ice into a coupe.

2. Garnish with a cucumber slice and an additional sprig of dill.

THE DORSEY

# – COCONUT WHITE RUSSIAN –

The Dorsey is located in The Venetian and specializes in all of the classic cocktails you can possibly think of. This is a perfect place to start your big night out on the town, when you've just freshened up and are still feeling elegant.

GLASSWARE: **Coupe**

GARNISH: **None**

- 1½ oz. Absolut Elyx
- 1½ oz. Caffe Lolita liqueur
- 1 oz. Coconut Cream, to top

1. Chill the coupe.

2. Add the vodka and liqueur to a cocktail shaker filled with ice, shake vigorously until chilled, and strain into the coupe.

3. Top with the Coconut Cream.

FOR COCONUT CREAM: Combine ½ oz. coconut syrup with 2 cups heavy cream and beat until stiff peaks form.

ELECTRA COCKTAIL CLUB

# – DISGRUNTLED MAI TAI –

A h, nothing says Vegas like a tasty mash-up of appropriated Tahitian traditions and a boozy, anise-flavored German digestif (Underberg).

GLASSWARE: **Rocks glass**

GARNISH: **Sprig of fresh mint and cocktail umbrella**

- **1 oz. Smith & Cross rum**
- **1 oz. Aperol**
- **1 oz. fresh lime juice**
- **½ oz. Orgeat**
- **½ oz. Curaçao**
- **Miniature bottle Underberg**

1. Add all of the ingredients, except for the Underberg, to a cocktail shaker filled with ice, shake vigorously until chilled, and strain over crushed ice into a rocks glass.

2. Carefully flip the bottle of Underberg into the cocktail so it is upside-down. Garnish with a sprig of mint and a cocktail umbrella.

ORGEAT: Preheat the oven to 400°F. Place 2 cups almonds on a baking sheet and toast in the oven for 5 minutes. Remove and let cool. Once cool, pulverize the nuts in a food processor, blender, or grain mill. Add the almond meal to a standard Simple Syrup (see page 15) after the sugar has dissolved. Remove the pan from heat and let the mixture stand for 3 to 6 hours. Strain the mixture through cheesecloth and discard the solids. Add 1 teaspoon rose water, 2 oz. vodka, and 1 tablespoon pure vanilla extract, stir to incorporate, and store in the refrigerator for up to 3 weeks.

## FAT TUESDAY

The popular Daquiri bar Fat Tuesday has several locations around The Strip. The drinks are massive, which is comforting—and dangerous—when walking around on a sweltering summer day. One of the most popular options at Fat Tuesday is the 44 Magnum, a mix of 190 Octane (vodka and orange juice) plus Cat 5 Hurricane (Bacardi 151 rum and white rum). Prepare yourself for a bit of a buzz. If you're feeling frisky, you could also grab a flavorful Mother Pucker Shot to enjoy on the side, or even add a shot of Everclear 151.

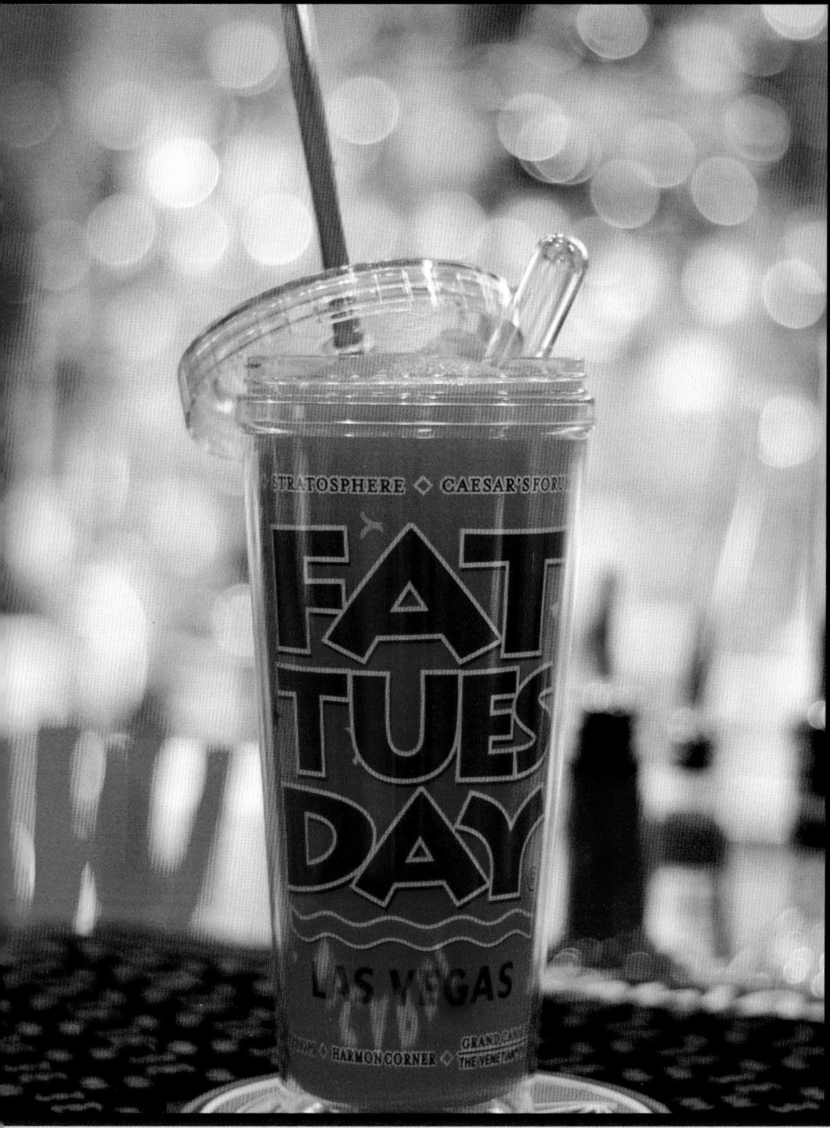
STRATOSPHERE
FAT TUESDAY
HARMON CORNER

# FLIGHTS

Located inside the Planet Hollywood Hotel, FLIGHTS serves fun, tapas-style comfort food. The name is a play on both its aviation theme as well as the flights of drinks offered at the establishment, such as the Cosmopolitan Flight (see page 69).

# – THE MAVERICK –

peachy take on a Whiskey Sour.

GLASSWARE: **Rocks glass**

GARNISH: **Sprig of fresh rosemary**

- ¼ oz. balsamic glaze
- ¾ oz. fresh lemon juice
- ¾ oz. Rosemary Syrup (see page 121)

- 1 oz. The Perfect Puree White Peach
- ½ oz. crème de pêche
- 1½ oz. bourbon

1. Add all of the ingredients to a cocktail shaker filled with ice, shake vigorously until chilled, and strain over ice into a rocks glass.

2. Garnish with the sprig of rosemary.

# – COSMOPOLITAN FLIGHT –

**M**ake a Cosmopolitan three ways with this tasting flight: classic, grapefruit, and orange. The method is the same for all three; only the fruit juices and garnishes change.

GLASSWARE: **Cocktail glass**
GARNISH: **Lime wheel, ¼ grapefruit wheel, ¼ orange wheel, respectively**

Classic:
- 1½ oz. Cosmo Mix
- 1 oz. vodka
- ¼ oz. fresh lime juice
- ½ oz. cranberry juice

Grapefruit:
- 1½ oz. Cosmo Mix
- 1 oz. vodka
- ¼ oz. fresh lime juice
- ½ oz. grapefruit juice

Orange:
- 1½ oz. Cosmo Mix
- 1 oz. vodka
- ¼ oz. fresh lime juice
- ½ oz. orange juice

1. Add all of the ingredients to a cocktail shaker filled with ice, shake vigorously until chilled, and strain into the cocktail glass.

2. Garnish with either a lime wheel, ¼ grapefruit wheel, or ¼ orange wheel, depending on which Cosmo you're making.

COSMO MIX: Combine 3 parts triple sec and 1 part Simple Syrup (see page 15).

# GHOST DONKEY

This Lower Manhattan mezcalería also has an outpost in Vegas. All you have to do is find the hidden blue door with a donkey on it inside The Cosmopolitan of Las Vegas.

# – MEZCAL SUN –

**M**ontelobos Mezcal is an artisanal spirit made in Santiago Matatlan, Oaxaca (Mexico). Founded by Ivan Saldana, Montelobos is made with 100 percent organic agave espadin, which takes about 8 to 12 years to mature. Fun fact: to ward off evil spirits, Montelobos' master distiller throws chili peppers into the fire when roasting the agave.

GLASSWARE: **Collins glass**

GARNISH: **Dehydrated lemon wheel (see page 166)**

- ¾ oz. Cabeza Tequila Blanco
- ¾ oz. Montelobos Mezcal
- 6 oz. tart orange juice
- ¾ oz. Hibiscus & Habanero Syrup (see page 57), to top

1. Add the tequila, mezcal, and tart orange juice to a Collins glass filled with ice and stir to combine.

2. Pour the syrup over the back of a spoon so that it settles on top of the drink and garnish with the dehydrated lemon wheel.

# – MOLE NEGRONI –

**M**ole recipes are often deeply guarded secrets, and, as bartender Ignacio "Nacho" Jimenez explains (see sidebar on page 74), mole recipes differ all over Mexico. So if you're not able to enjoy this rich riff on a classic Negroni at Ghost Donkey, make your own batch of mole at home, using a recipe that best suits your taste.

**GLASSWARE:** Rocks glass

**GARNISH:** Orange twist

- 1½ oz. Fidencio Clássico, fat-washed with mole paste and butter (see page 74)
- ¾ oz. Cynar
- ½ oz. Cocchi Storico Vermouth di Torino
- ½ oz. Rabarbaro Zucca
- 2 dashes Bittermens Mole Xocolatl Bitters

1. Add all of the ingredients to a mixing glass filled with ice, stir until chilled, and strain into a rocks glass filled with ice.

2. Garnish with the orange twist.

# INTERVIEW WITH
# IGNACIO "NACHO" JIMENEZ,
# GHOST DONKEY HEAD BARTENDER

**WHAT'S THE ORIGIN OF THE MOLE NEGRONI?**
The inspiration is mole, the quintessential Mexican dish. Always wanting to represent Mexican culture, we wanted to represent that ultimate dish and made it into a drink.

**WHAT EXACTLY IS MOLE?**
Mole it's, you know, it's just a sauce. Depends on the region of Mexico. You'll have different ingredients and different peppers. Some moles get up to a hundred different ingredients in them. It has anything from seeds to peppers to fruits, and bread.

**WHAT DOES THE MOLE NEGRONI PAIR WELL WITH?**
That's an interesting question. It's a great cocktail to finish your evening. If I have to pair it with something, I would say it would be right at the end of your dinner when you're probably thinking about getting dessert and thinking about getting something that helps you settle your belly. It has tons of amaro, actually two different amaros, in it so it will help with digestion.

**SO I GUESS THAT ANSWERS MY NEXT QUESTION ABOUT THE BEST TIME TO DRINK IT.**
We serve the Mole Negroni throughout the year, so it's not like there is a best season. I will say, going into the winter all these rich spices and peppers and fruits that go in there make more sense than in the summer. But people that typically try our Negroni just fall in love with it. It's so iconic because the taste is very unique and different. You have these rich flavors of the peppers and the chocolate and some of the fruit and banana notes and things that come along with it.

## FOR THE MOLE NEGRONI, HOW DO YOU INFUSE THE SPICES AND INGREDIENTS?

We fat-wash it. We didn't want to do a regular infusion, so we created a sauce. We crafted a paste of sesame seeds, pumpkin seeds, guajillo peppers, chipotle peppers, cocoa nibs, some black pepper, star anise, banana, figs, and raisins to create a paste, and we cook it with clarified butter. Then we infuse it with the mezcal for 24 hours, wait for the fat contents of the butter to rise, and then strain it.

## WHEN YOU INFUSE IT, DO YOU PUT IT IN THE REFRIGERATOR?

Yes. For us to remove the fat of the butter and for it to still be clear, we have to strain it through cheesecloth or a super-fine strainer.

GIADA

# – G –

**B**eautiful, sophisticated, approachable, and friendly, with a kick. If you're making this at home feel free to stencil any initial of your choosing with the bitters.

- **2 oz. Kappa Pisco**
- **¾ oz. Fee Brothers Pineapple Syrup**
- **¾ oz. fresh lime juice**
- **½ teaspoon apricot preserves**
- **1 drop Angostura Bitters**
- **1 oz. egg white**

1. Chill the coupe.

2. Add all of the ingredients to a cocktail shaker filled with ice, shake vigorously until chilled, and strain into the chilled coupe.

3. Using a stencil, spray bitters onto the foam to create your desired letter.

# – THE DESTROYER –

The sweet, almost-anise flavor of basil shines in this refreshing serve.

GLASSWARE: **Rocks glass**

GARNISH: **Fresh basil leaf and orange wheel**

- **2 strips orange peel**
- **4 large fresh basil leaves, torn**
- **1½ oz. Clase Azul Plata Tequila**
- **3 oz. tangerine juice**

1. Add the orange peels to a cocktail shaker and muddle. Add ice and the remaining ingredients.

2. Shake vigorously until chilled and then double-strain over ice into a rocks glass.

3. Garnish with an additional basil leaf and an orange wheel.

GREENE ST. KITCHEN

# – DOPE HAT –

As spice is a hard thing to regulate in cocktails, it helps to have some pro gear on your side, like an iSi Whipper, which for this drink gets filled with Jameson and 1½ oz. seeded jalapeño before being whipped for 3 minutes. The result brings out the pepper's botanical notes more than the heat it is known for. You can also do a more traditional infusion at home. Whichever approach you take, the spicy tickle at the back of your throat will leave you craving another sip.

GLASSWARE: **Rocks glass**

GARNISH: **Dehydrated blood orange wheel (see page 166), jalapeño pepper slices, and Fresno chili pepper slices**

---

- **1 oz. Jalapeño-Infused Jameson Irish Whiskey**
- **2 oz. agave nectar**
- **1 oz. blood orange juice**

1. Add all of the ingredients to a cocktail shaker filled with ice, shake vigorously until chilled, and strain over an ice sphere in a rocks glass.

2. Garnish with the dehydrated blood orange wheel and the slices of pepper.

JALAPEÑO-INFUSED JAMESON IRISH WHISKEY: Place 2 chopped jalapeño peppers in a 750 ml bottle of Jameson Irish Whiskey and steep for 24 hours. Strain before using or storing.

# – ROOK –

I f you're throwing a garden party and want to serve a drink that matches the theme, look no further, as the Rook resembles a potted plant. Minimal ingredients make this an easy but visually stunning drink to recreate at home.

GLASSWARE: **Flower pot (with no hole in the bottom)**
GARNISH: **Pineapple leaves, ground pink peppercorns,
and edible flowers**

- **2 oz. Hendrick's Gin**
- **1½ oz. Pesto Syrup**
- **1 oz. fresh lime juice**
- **Charcoal Water, to mist**

1. Combine all of the ingredients, except for the Charcoal Water, in a cocktail shaker filled with crushed ice, shake vigorously until chilled, and dump the contents of the shaker into the flower pot.

2. Add more crushed ice, mist with the Charcoal Water, and garnish with pineapple leaves, ground pink peppercorns, and edible flowers.

PESTO SYRUP: Add 1 tablespoon of each of the following: mint, basil, and thyme to a standard Simple Syrup (see page 15) after the sugar has dissolved and remove the saucepan from heat. Let cool completely and strain before using or storing.

CHARCOAL WATER: Add 1 gram of activated charcoal powder to 500 grams of mineral water, stir to combine, and pour the mixture into a spray bottle.

# SPOTLIGHT: ERIC HOBBIE

In 2001, Eric Hobbie began his journey as a bartender on New York City's club circuit. His first jobs in Las Vegas were at the Playboy Club, Jet, and Moon. His first restaurant employer in Vegas was Restaurant Charlie, owned by renowned chef Charlie Trotter. Hobbie secured a position at B&B and then Carnevino soon thereafter. There, he met his first true mentors, Pascal Bouldac and Victor Pinkston. Giada De Laurentis then approached him to design her beverage program and lead her very first restaurant concept. For the past two years, Hobbie has been running Clique Hospitality's entire beverage program, which at the time of writing includes 13 venues—though the group is continually growing.

As the winner of multiple national bartending competitions, one might expect Hobbie's conversation to be focused on his craft—the custom infusions, floral syrups, and other unique, palate-tingling items he's created during his career. Instead, talk about his guests dominates. Hobbie will tell you that bartending isn't about making the best cocktail. It's about making the guest feel as if they were being waited on by their own butler in their home, a butler who happens to be their best friend and has the best jokes and stories. It's about establishing a relationship as soon as the guest arrives and being able to bring them to a place they have never been before. As Hobbie says, "A good rapport between a bartender and their guests adds more to a cocktail than any ingredient you may put in."

When asked about the story behind the drinks menu at Greene St. Kitchen, Hobbie says, "Every menu I create has to have its own identity. It has to have a theme. Greene St. was one of my favorite projects because it hit home for me. Being from New York and growing up in its era of graffiti, and participating myself in its culture, made me feel like a kid again. The cocktails had to be as bright and full of life to match the restaurant. Even the cocktail names have a deep relation to the era. They are all graffiti slang terms. Graffiti is about big, bold statements and that's what the cocktails had to bring as well. There aren't many ingredients in each cocktail, but the flavors pack a punch and make their very own statement."

# – FAT CAP –

Sure, plain old pineapple juice will work in this recipe, but by adding some char to the pineapple before juicing it you'll be doing more than elementary cocktail making, you'll be ratcheting up the flavor of this sublime drink.

GLASSWARE: **Highball glass**

GARNISH: **Roasted pineapple chunk**

- 3 cucumber slices
- 2 oz. Casamigos Reposado Tequila
- 2 oz. Roasted Pineapple Juice
- 1 oz. agave nectar
- ½ oz. fresh lime juice

1. Add the cucumber slices to a cocktail shaker and muddle. Add ice and the remaining ingredients, shake vigorously until chilled, and strain into a highball glass filled with ice.

2. Garnish with the roasted pineapple chunk.

ROASTED PINEAPPLE JUICE: Grill or broil ¼-inch-thick slices of pineapple until they are caramelized on both sides. Reserve a chunk for garnish. If using a juicer, follow the juicer's instructions. If using a blender, puree the pineapple until it is smooth and then strain the puree, catching the juice in a bowl and pressing down on the solids to extract as much juice and flavor as possible.

# LIBERTINE SOCIAL

# – QUEEN'S PARK SWIZZLE –

Located inside Mandalay Bay Resort and Casino, Libertine Social emphasizes both being free of conventions and the power of food and drink to bring people together. Even if you think you don't like rum, this is a drink that needs to be tasted, and it can be made in large batches ahead of time, making it perfect for a party.

GLASSWARE: **Collins glass**

GARNISH: **Sprig of fresh mint**

- **14 fresh mint leaves**
- **1 oz. fresh lime juice**
- **1 oz. Simple Syrup (see page 15, use demerara sugar)**
- **2 oz. Angostura 7-Year-Old Rum**
- **10 dashes Angostura Bitters, to top**

1. Add the mint leaves to a Collins glass and muddle. Add the lime juice and syrup, fill the glass with crushed ice, add the rum, and use the swizzle method (see below) to combine the drink, adding more crushed ice as needed until the outside of the glass begins to frost.

2. Add additional crushed ice if desired, top with the bitters, and garnish with the sprig of mint.

SWIZZLE METHOD: Place a swizzle stick between your hands, lower the swizzle stick into the drink, and quickly rub your palms together to rotate the stick as you move it up and down in the drink. When frost appears on the outside of the vessel, the cocktail is ready to be enjoyed.

# – BARREL-AGED TONY NEGRONI –

This popular Italian cocktail may be a favorite for some, but many people find it to be an acquired taste. Bartender Tony Abou-Ganim says that the first time he tried it, he spit it right out. Now it is one of his favorite drinks, and the Barrel-Aged Tony Negroni is a huge hit at Libertine Social. What makes the Negroni so popular, according to Tony? The Libertine Social version of this drink isn't mixed traditionally. Tony's version is made from equal parts Campari, sweet vermouth, and gin that have been aged in a 10-liter oak barrel for 5 weeks before serving.

GLASSWARE: **Rocks glass**
GARNISH: **Strip of orange peel**

- **1 part Campari**
- **1 part Martini & Rossi Sweet Vermouth**
- **1 part Bombay Sapphire gin**

1. Add all of the ingredients to a mixing glass filled with ice, stir until chilled, and strain over a large block of ice into a rocks glass.

2. Garnish with the strip of orange peel.

# SPOTLIGHT: TONY ABOU-GANIM

Tony Abou-Ganim is a legendary bartender, often referred to as the "Modern Mixologist." You have probably seen him on *TODAY*, *Good Morning America*, CNBC, Fox News, and *Iron Chef America*, where he won three competitions for his cocktail pairings with food prepared by chefs Mario Batali, Jose Garces, and Shawn McClain.

Abou-Ganim, despite being a very busy man, has that uncanny ability to have a conversation and make you feel like you are the only person in the room, which is doubtless one of the reasons he is so successful. He treats every customer at the bar like he would friends in his home.

Abou-Ganim grew up in the bartending industry and learned from his cousin, Helen David. One of the first bartending jobs he had was at Harry Denton's, where he developed an appreciation for craft cock-

tails. Abou-Ganim spent some time in New York working at Babbo before moving to San Francisco to open the Starlight Room. At this point, it was still rare to go into a restaurant bar and be presented with a cocktail menu, but that didn't stop Abou-Ganim, who focused on fresh and from-scratch ingredients.

Around the beginning of the cocktail resurgence, Steve Wynn offered Abou-Ganim the chance to be part of a team that ended up influencing how Vegas drinks today. "There was this magical moment when everything aligned" he says. "I was very fortunate and blessed to be given the opportunity."

Once in Vegas, Abou-Ganim created the cocktail program at the Bellagio and mentored bartenders to embrace the types of beverage programs so common today. Fast-forward a few years and Abou-Ganim partnered with Levy Restaurants to design his signature craft cocktails for the T-Mobile Arena.

No matter what arena he's in, "I am always trying to improve the drinks, have some fun, and make sure my guests have a good experience," says Abou-Ganim.

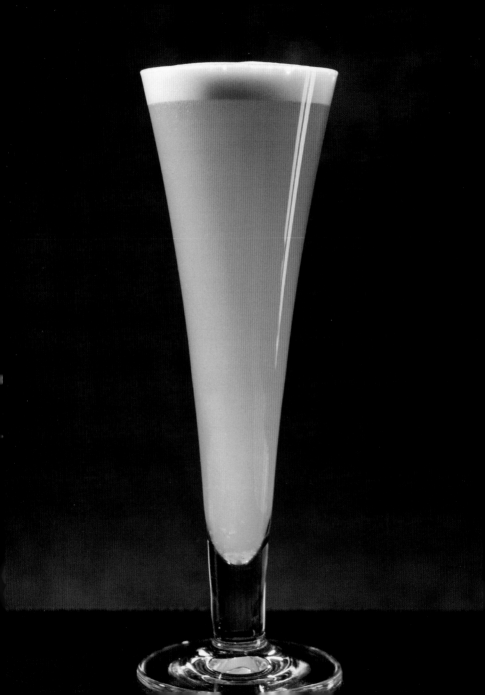

# – MILANO –

I f you're a fan of orange, especially blood orange, this is the cocktail for you.

GLASSWARE: **Champagne flute**

GARNISH: **None**

- 1½ oz. Effen Blood Orange Vodka
- ¾ oz. Aperol
- 1 oz. fresh lemon juice
- ½ oz. Simple Syrup (see page 15)
- ½ oz. egg white
- 1 oz. Prosecco, plus more to top, chilled

1. Chill a champagne flute.

2. Add all of the ingredients, except for the Prosecco, to a cocktail shaker containing 1 large ice cube and shake vigorously until chilled. Some prefer to dry shake the ingredients before adding ice.

3. Pour the Prosecco into the chilled glass and strain the cocktail into the glass.

4. Top with additional Prosecco, if needed.

MERCATO

# – NIGHT AT THE OPERA –

**E**very night at The Venetian, an aria, or some other operatic performance, takes place directly outside Mercato. Lead mixologist Robert Woods noticed that guests at the bar were so entranced by the singer that the bar now shuts off its music for 15 minutes every hour. The dramatic songs also inspired this drink. Cocktails and a show!

GLASSWARE: **Snifter**

GARNISH: **Filthy Black Cherry**

- **1½ oz. Woodford Reserve bourbon**
- **¾ oz. Carpano Antica Sweet Vermouth**
- **¾ oz. Lustau Pedro Ximénez Sherry**
- **2 dashes bitters**

1. Add all of the ingredients to a mixing glass filled with ice, stir until chilled, and strain into the snifter.

2. Garnish with the Filthy Black Cherry.

# SPOTLIGHT: ROBERT WOODS

What happens when your co-workers call off work and you're left handling an entire bar on your own? An opportunity to work in a brand-new restaurant at The Venetian. Robert Woods, bar manager and lead mixologist at Mercato, was definitely in the right place at the right time when he was working at his former bartending job at Olive Garden. The night his co-workers called out sick, scouts were going to every Olive Garden trying to find employees for Mercato.

Woods showed up early for his interview and was hired on the spot. However, he didn't start behind the bar. In fact, Woods was asked to serve even though he had never served a day in his life. Having no idea what to do, he quickly picked up on the necessary skills and worked his way up to a position behind the bar.

Woods is one of the most down-to-earth, kindhearted people you will ever meet. He will go the extra mile to make you smile.

He is also mega-talented. He can keep 10 drinks in his head at once, have a conversation going with everyone at his bar, and never lose his smile. While most people would be struggling to focus, Woods looks like he is having the time of his life. As does everyone else, sitting and enjoying his perfectly crafted cocktails.

# – ITALIAN HIGHBALL –

Created by Fabian Rubiano, this is an Italian drink with an American twist, hinged on a lip-smacking combination of bitter and sweet, which only seems fitting for a cocktail being served at a Venice-themed resort.

GLASSWARE: **Collins glass**
GARNISH: **Orange slice**

- 1½ oz. peach-flavored vodka
- ½ oz. Aperol
- ½ oz. white peach puree
- ½ oz. fresh lemon juice
- ½ oz. Simple Syrup (see page 15)
- Sanpellegrino Aranciata Rossa, to top

1. Add all of the ingredients, except the Sanpellegrino, to a cocktail shaker filled with ice, shake vigorously until chilled, and strain into a Collins glass filled with ice.

2. Top with the Sanpellegrino and garnish with the orange slice.

# – ACQUA DI VIDA –

A customer at Mercato demanded a rum drink, but not just any ol' rum drink, a blue one. After bar manager Robert Woods presented the on-the-spot creation to his guest, the man tried it and declared: "This made me feel alive again." Instantly, Woods connected the cocktail to the scene in *Pirates of the Caribbean: On Stranger Tides* where they found the fountain of youth. This one just happens to be Curaçao blue.

GLASSWARE: **Snifter**

GARNISH: **Filthy Black Cherry**

- 1 oz. Bacardi Silver
- 1 oz. Malibu rum
- 1½ oz. pineapple juice
- ¾ oz. Blue Curaçao
- ½ oz. Homemade Grenadine, to top

1. Add the rums and pineapple juice to a cocktail shaker filled with ice and shake vigorously for 10 seconds.

2. Add ice to the snifter. Pouring in a circular motion, coat the inside of the snifter with the Curaçao.

3. Strain the contents of the cocktail shaker into the snifter, top with the grenadine, and garnish with the Filthy Black Cherry.

FOR HOMEMADE GRENADINE: Combine 1 part Simple Syrup (see page 15) with 1 part juice from a jar of Filthy Black Cherries.

# MINUS5 ICE BAR

What better way to escape a Vegas summer scorcher than ducking into minus5 Ice Bar, where everything is made of ice, from the bar to the "glasses." There are three locations in Vegas, and they all offer up frosty cocktails while also featuring immersive activities like dynamic projection mapping and interactive ice experiences. There are, literally, hundreds of tons of ice created by a freezing process that includes a proprietary system that produces crystal-clear ice blocks known as "carvers' ice." Ice Bar maintains its consistently freezing temperature thanks to a state-of-the-art temperature monitoring system that accounts for ambient temperature, humidity, body temperature, and number of people in the space at any given time.

# – FROSTED BERRIES –

Fruity and light, this cocktail, like all drinks served at Ice Bar, gets colder the longer you take to finish it.

GLASSWARE: **Ice glass or chilled tumbler**

GARNISH: **None**

- 1 oz. Skyy Infusions Wild Strawberry Vodka
- ½ oz. peach schnapps
- 2½ oz. white cranberry juice

1. Build in the chosen glass and stir to combine.

# – NORTHERN LIGHTS –

This beautifully colored drink will transport you to the tundra—in the pleasant, peaceful sense.

GLASSWARE: **Ice glass or chilled tumbler**

GARNISH: **None**

- **1 oz. Blue Chair Bay White Rum**
- **1 oz. Midori**
- **2 oz. pineapple juice**

1. Build in the chosen glass and stir to combine.

# – MR. COCO –

Originally created at a dinner party in Las Vegas for an iconic personality and his billionaire friends, and inspired by a Scottish Westie, this exquisite alternative to a Piña Colada is this high-end bar's signature drink.

**GLASSWARE: Rocks glass**

**GARNISH: None**

- 1½ oz. Ciroc Coconut Vodka
- ¾ oz. Plantation XO 20th Anniversary Rum
- ¾ oz. Organic Mixology Coconut Lychee Berry Liqueur
- 2 oz. Liquid Alchemist Coconut Syrup
- ½ oz. fresh lemon juice
- 3 sprays Luxardo Amaretto-Angostura Bitters House Mix, to top

1. Add all of the ingredients, except for the house mix, to a cocktail shaker filled with ice, shake vigorously until chilled, and strain into a rocks glass filled with ice.

2. Top with the house mix.

**LUXARDO AMARETTO-ANGOSTURA BITTERS HOUSE MIX:**
Combine ¾ oz. Luxardo Amaretto with ¼ oz. Angostura Bitters and place the mixture in a spray bottle.

# – THE VICKY –

Created for a lovely philanthropist and socialite, who also happens to belong to one of the city's most influential and respected families, this delicious and exotic combination of rooibos tea, mandarin-infused vodka, and ginger liqueur is enriched with the silky mouthfeel of passion fruit foam.

GLASSWARE: **Coupe**

GARNISH: **Dehydrated baby pineapple wheel soaked in hibiscus syrup and sprayed with edible gold**

- 1½ oz. Hanson of Sonoma Organic Vodka Mandarin
- ¾ oz. Domaine de Canton
- 2 oz. brewed orange rooibos tea, chilled
- ½ oz. Pallini Limoncello
- 1 teaspoon Pedro Ximénez Sherry, to top
- Passion fruit foam, to top*

1. Chill the coupe.

2. Add all of the ingredients, except for the foam and Sherry, to a cocktail shaker filled with ice, shake vigorously until chilled, and strain into the chilled coupe.**

3. Add the Sherry with top with the passion fruit foam.

4. Garnish with a dehydrated baby pineapple wheel that has been soaked in hibiscus syrup and sprayed with edible gold.

*This is a proprietary recipe, so you'll have to hit Vegas to sip the real thing, or experiment at home until you get it right.

**At Mr. COCO they employ the Cuban roll method to mix this cocktail. For a proper roll, as per the bar's instructions: "Ice your tin to the top which will allow the julep strainer to perfectly sit on the top. Once you have enough ice, add your cocktail and begin by pouring from the tin to the speed cup (a mixing glass). When you begin to roll, raise both hands and pour from the big tin to the speed cup. Once you start pouring the cocktail from the tin to the speed cup, lower and raise the speed cup to complete the pour."

# SPOTLIGHT: FRANCESCO LAFRANCONI

Not only is Francesco Lafranconi a world-renowned mixologist, spirits industry educator, and icon of cocktail culture, he is the founder and managing partner of Mr. COCO, the visionary cocktail lounge at The Palms casino.

Under Lafranconi's leadership, MR. COCO provides guests with a modern luxury experience through sophisticated signature cocktails, well-paired dishes, intimate, world-class musical performances, and unmatched levels of service, significantly raising the bar for cocktail culture in Las Vegas.

Lafranconi's extensive knowledge and passion for his craft have made him a hit with his A-list celebrity clientele, notable corporate clients, Michelin-starred chefs, national restaurant chains, international hotel companies, and the thousands of people who've attended his seminars and live events around the world. His distinguished career also includes tenures at the helm of some of the world's leading hotel bars—The Gleneagles in Scotland; Gstaad Palace in Switzerland; The InterContinental in Cologne, Germany; and Harry's Bar at the Hotel Cipriani in Venice, Italy.

He has also won some of the world's most prestigious cocktail competitions, including the Bacardi-Martini Grand Prix World Final and John White Course in Singapore (both involving the International Bartenders Association), the Bartender Hall of Fame Award from *Bartender Magazine*, the Raising the Bar Award from *Cheers Magazine*, Mixologist of the Year from *Nightclub and Bar Magazine*, Tales of the Cocktail's Golden Spirit Award, and Best In Show at the Iron Mixologist Competition, which was sponsored by Wine & Spirits Wholesalers of America.

But Lafranconi's proudest achievement is founding the Academy of Spirits and Fine Service in 2000. The 12-week education program has trained over 1,000 beverage professionals, instilling in them the same enthusiasm Lafranconi brings to every cocktail. He is also the proud inventor of the bar work station known as "the racetrack," which is poised to revolutionize the beverage industry.

As a consummate connoisseur and industry ambassador who is passionate about sharing his knowledge with everyone he meets, Lafranconi is known worldwide by his motto: "We're not drinking, we're learning."

# – NEGRONI BIANCO –

A great alternative to the one and only Negroni! The Bianco uses Aviation American Gin for its more subtle flavor, which perfectly intertwines with the complexity of Luxardo Bitter Bianco and the citrus-forward taste of Italicus.

**GLASSWARE:** Tumbler

**GARNISH:** Strips of grapefruit and lemon peel
skewered on a cocktail pick

- 1 oz. Aviation American Gin
- 1 oz. Luxardo Bitter Bianco
- 1 oz. Italicus Rosolio di Bergamotto
- ½ oz. Fusion Napa Valley Verjus Blanc

1. Add all of the ingredients to a mixing glass filled with ice and stir until chilled.

2. Strain into a tumbler containing a large block of ice and garnish with the skewered citrus peels.

ROSINA

# – BANCO DE MEXICO –

The menu at this bar in the Palazzo includes a classic Mint Julep, but if you are in the know, be sure to try one of the off-the-menu "secret juleps," built around spirits like rye, brandy, and tequila. This serve is one of those secrets, proof of the old adage that knowledge is power.

GLASSWARE: **Copper mug**

GARNISH: **Confectioners' sugar and sprig of fresh mint**

- **1½ oz. añejo tequila**
- **½ oz. mezcal**

- **½ oz. crème de cacao**
- **Rose water, to mist**

1. Add all of the ingredients, except for the rose water, to a copper mug filled with crushed ice and stir to combine.

2. Spray rose water over the top and garnish with confectioners' sugar and a sprig of mint.

SAKE ROK

# — SARU 47 —

Tommy Schimmel and the Sake Rok team created this fun drink, which demands attention with its flaming lemon peel.

GLASSWARE: **Cocktail glass**

GARNISH: **Sprig of fresh lavender**

- 1 oz. Source One Single Estate Vodka
- 1 oz. Monkey 47 Schwarzwald Gin
- ½ oz. Dolin Genepy le Chamois
- ½ oz. Honey Syrup (see page 185)
- 1 strip lemon peel

1. Chill the cocktail glass.

2. Add all of the ingredients, except for the lemon peel, to a cocktail shaker filled with ice, shake vigorously until chilled, and strain into the chilled cocktail glass.

3. Using extreme care, hold a lit match or a lighter beneath the lemon peel and pinch it so that it releases its oil over the flame and cocktail.

4. Garnish with the sprig of lavender.

# – OLD SMOKEY KNIGHTS –

Old Smokey Knights does battle with the Saru 47 (see page 117) for the title of Sake Rok's signature cocktail. It pairs perfectly with my favorites off the food menu: Hamachi Ceviche and Sake ROK Sliders.

**GLASSWARE: Rocks glass**

**GARNISH: Strip of grapefruit peel**

- 1½ oz. Cazadores Reposado Tequila
- ½ oz. El Silencio Espadin Mezcal
- ¾ oz. Simple Syrup (see page 15)
- 4 dashes Angostura Orange Bitters

1. Add all of the ingredients to a mixing glass filled with ice, stir until chilled, and strain into a rocks glass filled with ice.

2. Garnish with the strip of grapefruit peel.

# – WALK THIS WAY –

With only four ingredients and no garnish, this cocktail is all about the subtle rosemary aroma and the Kikori Whiskey, which is light in color, similar to a Pinot Grigio.

GLASSWARE: **Coupe**

GARNISH: **None**

- 2 oz. Kikori Whiskey
- ½ oz. sweet vermouth
- ½ oz. dry vermouth
- ¾ oz. Rosemary Syrup

1. Add all of the ingredients to a mixing glass filled with ice, stir until chilled, and strain into the coupe.

ROSEMARY SYRUP: Add 10 sprigs of fresh rosemary (per quart) to a standard Simple Syrup (see page 15) after the sugar has dissolved. Remove the pan from heat and cover. Let cool completely and strain before using or storing.

## SCOTCH 80 PRIME

This upscale steakhouse in The Palms has a $3 million whiskey selection that is as impressive as the Basquiats on the wall.

# – UTOPIA –

**A** perfect combination of pear, walnut, and vanilla bean. This very simple, yet warm and velvety blend is a perfect addition to any cocktail party!

GLASSWARE: **Rocks glass**

GARNISH: **Dehydrated apple slice**

- 1½ oz. Redemption Rye Whiskey
- ½ oz. St. George Spiced Pear Liqueur
- ½ oz. Vanilla Syrup
- 2 dashes Fee Brothers Black Walnut Bitters

1. Add all of the ingredients to a mixing glass filled with ice, stir until chilled, and strain into a rocks glass containing a large block of ice.

2. Garnish with the dehydrated apple slice.

VANILLA SYRUP: Add 2 split vanilla bean pods or 2 tablespoons pure vanilla extract to a standard Simple Syrup (see page 15) after the sugar has dissolved. Remove from heat and let cool. If using vanilla bean pods, strain before using or storing.

# – BUOL MULE –

Replacing vodka with whisky is a great way to change up the cocktail we all know and love. You can use any Scotch, but Johnnie Walker Black will turn everyone's head.

**GLASSWARE:** Copper mug

**GARNISH:** Fresh mint leaves and lime wheel

• 1½ oz. Johnnie Walker Black
• ½ oz. hibiscus honey
• 1 oz. Perricone Farms Fresh Lime Juice
• 2 oz. Fever-Tree Ginger Beer, to top

1. Add all of the ingredients, except for the ginger beer, to a cocktail shaker filled with ice, shake vigorously until chilled, and strain into a copper mug filled with ice.

2. Top with the ginger beer, gently stir, and garnish with mint leaves.

# – LEVEL 55: GHOSTBAR –

When you order this drink at Scotch 80 Prime, it's poured table-side from a carafe set in dry ice. It's quite a spectacle, and the show doesn't stop there.

GLASSWARE: **Coupe**

GARNISH: **Fresh mint leaves**

- **5 fresh mint leaves**
- **1½ oz. Empress 1908 Indigo Gin**
- **Juice of 1 lemon**
- **½ oz. Italicus Rosolio di Bergamotto**
- **2 dashes orange bitters**

1. Add the mint leaves to a cocktail shaker and muddle. Add ice and the remaining ingredients, shake vigorously until chilled, and double-strain into the coupe.

2. Garnish with additional mint leaves.

STK

# – STRAWBERRY COBBLER –

The Strawberry Cobbler, just like a summer-ripe strawberry, is perfectly sweet with a subtle tartness.

**GLASSWARE: Cocktail glass**

**GARNISH: None**

- **Graham cracker crumbs, for the rim**
- **2 strawberries**
- **2 oz. vodka**
- **¼ oz. Simple Syrup (see page 15)**
- **1 oz. sour mix (see page 177 for homemade)**

1. Wet the rim of the cocktail glass and dip it into the graham cracker crumbs.

2. Add the strawberries to a cocktail shaker and muddle. Add ice and the remaining ingredients, shake vigorously until chilled, and strain into the glass.

# – CUCUMBER STILETTO –

**E**specially refreshing in the summer, make sure you have enough ingredients on hand so you can make several, as one is never enough.

GLASSWARE: **Cocktail glass**

GARNISH: **Cucumber slice**

- **2 cucumber slices**
- **6 fresh mint leaves**
- **¾ oz. fresh lime juice**
- **¾ oz. Simple Syrup (see page 15)**
- **1½ oz. Ketel One Citroen**
- **¾ oz. St-Germain**

1. Add the cucumber, mint, lime juice, and simple syrup to a cocktail shaker and muddle.

2. Add the vodka, St-Germain, and ice, shake vigorously until chilled, and strain into the cocktail glass.

3. Garnish with an additional slice of cucumber.

# – SPICE OF LOVE –

F or those who like it hot, this is the drink for you, thanks to the muddled jalapeños.

GLASSWARE: **Cocktail glass**

GARNISH: **Jalapeño pepper slice**

- **2 jalapeño pepper slices**
- **1 teaspoon sugar**
- **1 splash sour mix (see page 177 for homemade)**

- **2 oz. premium vodka**
- **1 oz. passion fruit puree**
- **½ oz. mango juice**

1. Add the jalapeños and sugar to a cocktail shaker and muddle.

2. Add ice and the remaining ingredients, shake vigorously until chilled, and double-strain into the cocktail glass.

3. Garnish with an additional slice of jalapeño.

# – RUM 'N' BRAMBLE –

**B**asil is a nice addition to a number of summer cocktails, but the Rum 'n' Bramble shows that it and rum aren't restricted to the warm weather.

**GLASSWARE:** Collins glass

**GARNISH:** Fresh basil leaf and strip of lemon peel

---

- **2 oz. Santa Teresa 1796 Rum**
- **1 oz. yuzu juice**
- **½ oz. dry vermouth**
- **1 oz. agave nectar**

- **2 oz. blackberry puree (see page 155 for homemade)**
- **1 dash cardamom bitters**
- **4 fresh basil leaves**

**1.** Add all of the ingredients to a cocktail shaker filled with ice, shake vigorously until chilled, and double-strain into a Collins glass filled with ice.

**2.** Garnish with an additional basil leaf and a strip of lemon peel.

T-MOBILE ARENA

# — ATOMIC FIZZ —

The Las Vegas Valley has finally been graced with a professional sports team, and boy, oh boy are the locals happy. The T-Mobile Arena is home to the Golden Knights—an NHL team that was a smash hit right away, making it all the way to the Stanley Cup Finals in its inaugural season. Mixologist Tony Abou-Ganim (see pages 92–93) and Levy Restaurants worked together to create a signature beverage, the Atomic Fizz, which is a nod to the atomic history in Vegas. Like so much in the city, the drink's bright magenta hue does not go unnoticed.

GLASSWARE: **Collins glass**

GARNISH: **Fan of lemon slices**

- 2 oz. Absolut Citron
- 1 oz. Aperol
- 1½ oz. fresh lemon juice
- 1 oz. agave nectar
- ½ oz. prickly pear puree
- 1 oz. Q Soda Water, chilled, to top

1. Add all of the ingredients, except for the soda water, to a cocktail shaker filled with ice, shake vigorously until chilled, and strain into a Collins glass filled with ice.

2. Top with the soda water and garnish with a fan of lemon slices.

# – SCRATCH MARGARITA –

**A**t any big sporting event or concert, you have to wait in line for food and drinks at the T-Mobile. If my informal polling is correct, this has to be one of the most popular beverages on offer at the arena. Avoid the lines and make it at home.

GLASSWARE: **Rocks glass**

GARNISH: **Lime wedge**

---

- **2 oz. silver tequila**
- **1 oz. Cointreau**

- **2 oz. sour mix (see page 177 for homemade)**
- **1 oz. fresh lime juice**

1. Add all of the ingredients to a cocktail shaker filled with ice, shake vigorously until chilled, and strain over ice into a rocks glass.

2. Garnish with the lime wedge.

# – BEHOLD THE GOLD –

**B**ehold the Gold. Golden Knights. Get it?

**GLASSWARE: Rocks glass**

**GARNISH: Dehydrated pineapple cross**

- ◆ 2 oz. reposado tequila
- ◆ 1 oz. Domaine de Canton
- ◆ 1 oz. pineapple juice
- ◆ 1 oz. fresh lemon juice
- ◆ ½ oz. passion fruit puree
- ◆ 1 oz. agave nectar

1. Add all of the ingredients to a cocktail shaker filled with ice, shake vigorously until chilled, and strain over ice into a rocks glass.

2. Garnish with the dehydrated pineapple cross.

TERRAZA

# – OWEN'S MEGA MULE –

This is a party punch. Owen's Craft Mixers are heavily featured at Terraza due to their high quality, and can be found nationwide in restaurants, bars, and retailers.

GLASSWARE: **12 copper mugs**

GARNISH: **Lime wheels**

- **1 (750 ml) bottle New Amsterdam Vodka**
- **1½ (750 ml) bottles Owen's Craft Mixers Ginger Beer + Lime**

1. Fill the mugs with ice.

2. Add the ingredients to a punch bowl, stir to combine, and then ladle into the mugs.

3. Garnish with the lime wheels and offer straws for serving.

# – PINK JASMINE MARTINI –

attersall is a liqueur made with aromatic flowers, making it a perfect partner for the Bloom Jasmine & Rose Gin.

**GLASSWARE:** Cocktail glass
**GARNISH:** Edible orchid blossom

- Pink sugar, for the rim
- 2 oz. Bloom Jasmine & Rose Gin
- 1 squeeze fresh lime juice
- ¼ oz. Tattersall Crème de Fleur

1. Wet the rim of the cocktail glass and dip it into the pink sugar.

2. Add the remaining ingredients to a cocktail shaker filled with ice, shake vigorously until chilled, and strain into the glass.

3. Garnish with the edible orchid blossom.

# – OWEN'S SPRITZ –

This cocktail is a great way to use the beguiling flavor of Aperol.

GLASSWARE: **Wine glass**

GARNISH: **Orange slice**

- 1½ oz. New Amsterdam Vodka
- ¼ oz. Aperol
- Owen's Craft Mixers Grapefruit + Lime, to top

1. Add the vodka and Aperol to a wine glass filled with ice and stir to combine.

2. Top with the mixer and garnish with the orange slice.

VETRI CUCINA

For those who gravitate towards a soft, floral, fruity drink, this *aperitivo* is the way to go. Mixologist David Cooper loves this cocktail, not only because of his loyalty to the Nolet family, but because it is an excellent stage for gin. "It's almost like taking an Aperol spritz but with a cocktail twist," says Cooper.

**GLASSWARE: Coupe**

**GARNISH: Strip of lemon peel**

- **Sea salt, for the rim**
- **2 oz. Nolet Silver Gin**
- **1½ oz. fresh grapefruit juice**
- **¾ oz. Aperol**

1. Wet one-third of the coupe's rim and dip it into the sea salt.

2. Add the remaining ingredients to a cocktail shaker filled with ice, shake vigorously until chilled, and then strain into the coupe.

3. Garnish with the strip of lemon peel.

# – IL GEORGIO –

Cooper owes a big thanks to George Clooney and his success with Casamigos for this fun cocktail. The Il Georgio is a spicy, Italian-inflected Margarita, and in Cooper's words it's "an all-day, every-day drink."

**GLASSWARE:** Rocks glass

**GARNISH:** Strip of orange peel

- Tajín, for the rim
- 2 oz. Casamigos Reposado Tequila
- ½ oz. Amaro Meletti
- ½ oz. Domaine de Canton
- ½ oz. Aperol
- ¾ oz. fresh lime juice

1. Wet half of the rocks glass's rim, dip it into the Tajín, and then add ice.

2. Add the remaining ingredients to a cocktail shaker filled with ice, shake vigorously until chilled, and strain into the glass.

3. Garnish with the strip of orange peel.

# SPOTLIGHT: DAVID COOPER

Don't expect to order a cocktail at Vetri Cucina without meeting the man behind the bar. David Cooper or "Coop," as many locals know him, will make sure to personally introduce himself to anyone ordering one of his specialty cocktails. "I will make my way over to wherever you are sitting and ask you which spirit you prefer," says Cooper. With over 40 years of experience in this industry, he knows how to read the room, and has a knack for making everyone around him feel comfortable. That talent doesn't just extend to the customers, it's even apparent with his staff.

If you've never heard of Cooper, the only thing you need to know is that he is an industry badass. He got his start working for his dad, making cocktails whenever someone wouldn't show up for work. Just 16 at the time, he's thankful that he got his foot in the door that early.

The first thing he teaches new hires is that they have a circle of trust. "I always say to take what you like, throw away what you don't." Cooper and his staff have definitely created a circle of trust and, in this industry, it's a must. "This profession can get weird and there is always someone that wants your job, but if you keep a close-knit family and give them the trust, everyone will win."

While Cooper has built a very successful life in this busy city, he is also a family man. If you ever go into Vetri Cucina and don't see Coop, you best believe he is spending time with his family, in conversation with one or all of children (two sons and a daughter), and two granddaughters, with the talk ranging from UFOs to religion and, of course, cocktails.

If you plan on letting Cooper guide your cocktail selections during a meal at Vetri Cucina, expect your evening to look something like his: a nice aperitivo to get the night going, followed by a cocktail like the Italian Old Fashioned. Then, enjoy your appetizers, dinner, and maybe a glass or two of whichever wine you prefer. Lastly, you'll end the night with an amaro, which will ensure that you are neither full nor tired, and head out the door with good feelings intact.

If you're ever out and not sure what to order, Cooper suggests choosing a cocktail with five ingredients or less. No need to worry if something is muddled, strained, or double-foamed. And find a cocktail that allows you to taste the ingredients. However, venture out of your comfort zone a bit and order something you would never normally gravitate toward. Amaro cocktails are a great option for getting a little adventurous, according to Cooper.

This is the best-selling cocktail at Vetri Cucina. This is your girls' night out (or in) Cosmo on steroids.

**GLASSWARE: Coupe**

**GARNISH: Strip of orange peel**

- 1½ oz. Ketel One Orange & Peach Blossom Vodka
- ¼ oz. Patron Citronge Mango
- ½ oz. Cointreau
- ½ oz. fresh lime juice
- 1 oz. blood orange juice
- ½ oz. egg white or aquafaba (see page 300)

1. Chill the coupe.

2. Add all of the ingredients to a cocktail shaker filled with ice and shake vigorously until chilled. Strain the cocktail into a glass and discard the ice. Return the cocktail to the shaker and dry shake for 10 seconds.

3. Pour the cocktail into the chilled coupe and garnish with the strip of orange peel.

YARDBIRD

# – BLACKBERRY BOURBON – LEMONADE

Cardamom is a polarizing flavor—people either love its floral sweetness or love to hate it. It's very subtle here, as the Wild Turkey is what really stands out.

GLASSWARE: 16 oz. mason jar

GARNISH: Lemon wheel and blackberry

- 1 dash Angostura Bitters
- 1 cardamom pod
- 1½ oz. Wild Turkey 81 Bourbon
- ¾ oz. fresh lemon juice
- ¾ oz. Simple Syrup (see page 15)
- ½ oz. Blackberry Puree
- ½ oz. soda water, to top

1. Add all of the ingredients, except for the soda water, to a cocktail shaker filled with ice, shake vigorously until chilled, and pour the contents of the shaker into a mason jar.

2. Top with the soda water and garnish with a lemon wheel and a blackberry.

BLACKBERRY PUREE: Place 1 pint of blackberries in a food processor and puree. Strain through a piece of cheesecloth or a fine sieve before using.

# – SOUTHERN REVIVAL –

Sometimes, no matter where you are, you just need some of that sweet, sweet Kentucky bourbon.

GLASSWARE: **16 oz. mason jar**

GARNISH: **Red grapes and fresh basil leaves**

- **3 fresh basil leaves**
- **1½ oz. Old Forester 86 bourbon**
- **¾ oz. Simple Syrup (see page 15)**
- **½ oz. fresh lemon juice**
- **½ oz. ginger ale, to top**

1. Add all of the ingredients, except for the ginger ale, to a cocktail shaker filled with ice, shake vigorously until chilled, and pour the contents of the shaker into a mason jar.

2. Top with the ginger ale and garnish with red grapes and additional basil leaves.

# – YARDBIRD OLD FASHIONED –

The caramel notes in the Wild Turkey go very nicely with the maple syrup.

GLASSWARE: **Rocks glass**

GARNISH: **Strip of orange peel**

- **2 dashes Angostura Bitters**
- **2 dashes orange bitters**
- **2 oz. Wild Turkey 81 Bourbon**
- **¼ oz. real maple syrup**

1. Add all of the ingredients to a mixing glass filled with ice, stir until chilled, and strain over an ice sphere into a rocks glass.

2. Garnish with the strip of orange peel.

# OFF THE STRIP

I PLUM FORGOT • PRETTY IN PINK • LIMEY SON OF A GUN • JACQUELINE'S REVENGE • SIDECAR • CLARIFIED MILK PUNCH • STRIP TINI • PINEAPPLE UNDER THE SEA • JARDÍN FRESCO • BERRETTO DA NOTTE • CATALUNYA • EDO GIN & TONIC • TONGA REEFER • DEMON RHUMBA • SCURVY • BIRDS OF PARADISE • HIBISCUS COSMO • BLUEBERRY KOMBUCHA MOJITO • THANK YOU VERY MATCHA • ELIZABETH'S GIN & TONIC • THE MIDNIGHT RAMBLER • ALEX & PIPER • SPIKED LIMONANA • VEGAS HEART • ADIOS MOTHER F'ER • BRUNCH IN MILAN • MANGO MARTINI • UNICORNS & SUNSHINE • BREAK THE RULES • MILKY WAY MARTINI • SPARK PLUG • MONKEY'S AVIATION • VGK PUCK DROP • CAMPFIRE S'MORES • BUTTERFLY BITTER • SINK THE PINK • LET IT HAPPEN • F*CK THE PAIN AWAY • ELEPHANT IN THE ROOM • DON'T CRY WOLF • SCROOGE McDUCK • GOURMET LEMON • BLUE MARINER

**M**any visitors to Las Vegas do not know that there's life beyond The Strip. Red Rock Canyon National Conservation Area is just one of the many beautiful places to visit while in Vegas, featuring hiking trails, a scenic drive, and seasonal waterfalls. And did I mention all the bars and restaurants?

ADA'S

# – I PLUM FORGOT –

T he wine cooler to end all your worries, thanks to brachetto, the sweet Italian grape that lends its talents to this drink's topper.

GLASSWARE: **Rocks glass**

GARNISH: **Plum Flower**

- ◆ **2 oz. bourbon**
- ◆ **1 oz. Plum Syrup**
- ◆ **½ oz. Amaro Pasubio**
- ◆ **Brachetto d'Acqui, to top**

1. Add the bourbon, syrup, and Amaro to a cocktail shaker filled with ice, shake vigorously until chilled, and double-strain over ice into a rocks glass.

2. Top with the Brachetto and garnish with the Plum Flower.

PLUM SYRUP: Place 1 cup plum juice, 1 cup sugar, and 1 tablespoon fresh lemon juice in a saucepan and bring to a simmer, stirring until the sugar has dissolved. Remove from heat and let cool completely before using or storing.

PLUM FLOWER: Use fresh plum round slices, curled up to resemble a rosette and then placed on a skewer or a stick.

Grapefruit is a fun citrus to work with since its taste ranges from sharply bitter to sweet and sugary. The Pretty in Pink is a perfect stage to show off these various talents.

GLASSWARE: **Wine glass**

GARNISH: **Roasted Grapefruit Wheel**

- **2½ oz. Malfy Gin Rosa**
- **4 dashes grapefruit bitters**
- **½ oz. Bittermilk Charred Grapefruit Tonic**

1. Add all of the ingredients to a mixing glass filled with ice and stir until chilled.

2. Strain over ice into a wine glass and garnish with the Roasted Grapefruit Wheel.

ROASTED GRAPEFRUIT WHEEL: Preheat the oven to 425°F. Thinly slice a grapefruit and place the slices on a baking sheet lined with parchment paper. Roast in the oven for 10 to 15 minutes, until the fruit starts to caramelize. Remove and let cool before using. Don't be afraid to try this with other citrus fruits as well.

# – LIMEY SON OF A GUN –

Salers Aperitif is a very versatile liqueur that can be enjoyed on the rocks or with a touch of citrus. It also fits well in cocktails, as it adds earthy, bitter, and floral notes.

GLASSWARE: **Coupe**

GARNISH: **Lime twist**

- 1½ oz. Principe de los Apostoles Gin
- ¾ oz. Lime Cordial
- ½ oz. Salers Gentiane Aperitif
- 4 dashes lime bitters

1. Add all of the ingredients to a mixing glass filled with ice, stir until chilled, and strain into the coupe.

2. Garnish with the lime twist.

LIME CORDIAL: In a large pot, combine 2 quarts lime husks, 4 quarts sugar, and 2 quarts water and boil until the sugar has dissolved and the mixture is syrupy. Remove pot from heat, add 4¼ oz. of vodka, cover, and let sit for 72 hours. Strain before using or storing.

# – JACQUELINE'S REVENGE –

This exceptionally flavorful and ultra-crisp drink is ideal for sipping by the pool in the gleaming sunlight.

GLASSWARE: **Rocks glass**

GARNISH: **Filthy Black Cherry**

- 1½ oz. bourbon
- ½ oz. Simple Syrup (see page 15)
- ¼ oz. Ancho Reyes
- ¼ oz. sweet vermouth
- 1 dash chocolate bitters
- 1 oz. apple juice

1. Add all of the ingredients to a cocktail shaker filled with ice in the order they are listed, shake vigorously until chilled, and then strain the cocktail over ice into a rocks glass.

2. Garnish with the Filthy Black Cherry.

A true classic that you can tailor to your taste depending on the orange liqueur you choose. Some are drier, others are sweet—the task here is to find one that suits you.

**GLASSWARE:** Cocktail glass

**GARNISH:** Lemon twist

- Sugar, for the rim
- 2 oz. Hennessy VSOP
- ¾ oz. fresh lemon juice
- ¾ oz. orange liqueur

1. Wet the rim of the cocktail glass and dip it into the sugar.

2. Add the remaining ingredients to a cocktail shaker filled with ice, shake vigorously until chilled, and strain into the cocktail glass.

3. Garnish with the lemon twist.

# – CLARIFIED MILK PUNCH –

A batched version of the Americana's signature drink, making it ideal for a party.

GLASSWARE: **Rocks glasses**
GARNISH: **Strips of orange peel**

- 8½ cups gin
- 8 cups sugar
- 8 cups hot water
- 2 cups honey
- 8 cups brewed Earl Grey tea
- 2 cups brandy

- 8 cups milk
- 1 teaspoon pure vanilla extract
- Zest of 6 lemons
- 6 dashes bitters

1. Add all of the ingredients to a large saucepan and warm over medium heat, stirring until the honey has been completely incorporated.

2. Strain through a piece of cheesecloth to remove impurities or curdled milk. This leaves you with a smooth, creamy cocktail that is not too heavy. Let the punch cool.

3. To serve, ladle the punch over a block of ice into a rocks glass and let it sit for 30 seconds. Express a strip of orange peel over each cocktail and then drop it into the drink as a garnish.

**BAR CODE**

# – STRIP TINI –

Named after the famed Vegas Strip and the classic Martini cocktail, this playful serve is always available at this burger bar that never closes. If you happen to be there in the morning and aren't in the mood for a Strip Tini, order the Secret Ingredient Bloody Mary.

GLASSWARE: **Cocktail glass**
GARNISH: **Slice of strawberry**

- **Sugar, for the rim**
- **1 strawberry**
- **1 oz. Skyy Infusions Wild Strawberry Vodka**

- **½ oz. St-Germain**
- **4 oz. Sour Mix**

1. Wet the rim of the cocktail glass and dip it into the sugar.

2. Add the strawberry to a cocktail shaker and muddle. Add ice and the remaining ingredients, shake vigorously until chilled, and strain into the cocktail glass.

3. Garnish with the slice of strawberry.

SOUR MIX: Place 1 cup sugar and 1 cup water in a saucepan and bring to a boil, stirring until the sugar has dissolved. Remove from heat and let cool. Add 1 cup strained fresh lemon juice and ½ cup strained fresh lime juice to the syrup and stir to incorporate. Use immediately or store in the refrigerator.

# – PINEAPPLE UNDER THE SEA –

**B**orn and Raised is the official bar of the Vegas Golden Knights, and it is crazy during the hockey season. If you can't make it to a game at the T-Mobile Arena, this is the place to be. The award-winning, made-from-scratch menu is delicious, as are all of the specialty cocktails.

GLASSWARE: **Collins glass**

GARNISH: **Chunk of candied pineapple and maraschino cherry**

- 1 oz. Absolut Elyx
- 1 oz. Malibu
- ½ oz. Torani Vanilla Syrup
- 1 oz. fresh lemon juice
- 3 oz. pineapple Juice

1. Add all of the ingredients to a cocktail shaker filled with ice, shake vigorously until chilled, and strain over ice into a Collins glass.

2. Garnish with a chunk of candied pineapple and a maraschino cherry.

BORRACHA

# – JARDÍN FRESCO –

E ven if you elect to eschew the jalapeño, there is no denying the wonderfully vegetal quality of this cocktail, which is brought to life by the Prosecco float.

GLASSWARE: **Margarita coupe**

GARNISH: **Cucumber slice and sprig of fresh cilantro**

- **5 cucumber slices**
- **1 jalapeño pepper slice (optional)**
- **1 sprig of fresh cilantro**
- **1½ oz. Casamigos Blanco Tequila**

- **¾ oz. St-Germain**
- **1 oz. fresh lime juice**
- **2 oz. Prosecco, to float**

1. Add the cucumber, jalapeño (if using), and cilantro to a cocktail shaker and muddle.

2. Add ice and the tequila, St-Germain, and lime juice, shake vigorously until chilled, and double-strain into the Margarita coupe.

3. Pour the Prosecco over the back of a spoon so that it floats on top of the cocktail and garnish with a slice of cucumber and an additional sprig of cilantro.

## BOTTIGLIA

True, Bottiglia is not exactly in Las Vegas. It is technically in Henderson, but sits so close to The Strip that you still feel part of the city when you're there. Perhaps that feeling explains the odd rivalry between Henderson and Vegas.

# − BERRETTO DA NOTTE −

I f you cannot get your hands on blood oranges for the Blood Orange Sorbet, feel free to use regular oranges, tangerines, or grapefruits. This one is great for a fun night at home with the girls.

GLASSWARE: **Champagne flute**

GARNISH: **Dehydrated blood orange wheel (see page 166) and sprig of fresh mint**

- 1 oz. St-Germain
- ¼ oz. fresh lemon Juice
- 3 oz. Prosecco
- 1 scoop Blood Orange Sorbet

1. Pour the St-Germain, lemon juice, and Prosecco into the champagne flute.

2. Place the scoop of sorbet on top and garnish with a dehydrated blood orange wheel and a sprig of mint.

BLOOD ORANGE SORBET: Making sorbet is easy, so long as you have an ice cream maker. Place 1 cup fresh blood orange juice and ¾ cup sugar in a saucepan and warm over low heat, stirring until the sugar has dissolved. Remove from heat and then stir in 2 more cups of fresh blood orange juice. Refrigerate for 4 hours and turn into sorbet per ice cream maker's instructions.

# EDO TAPAS & WINE

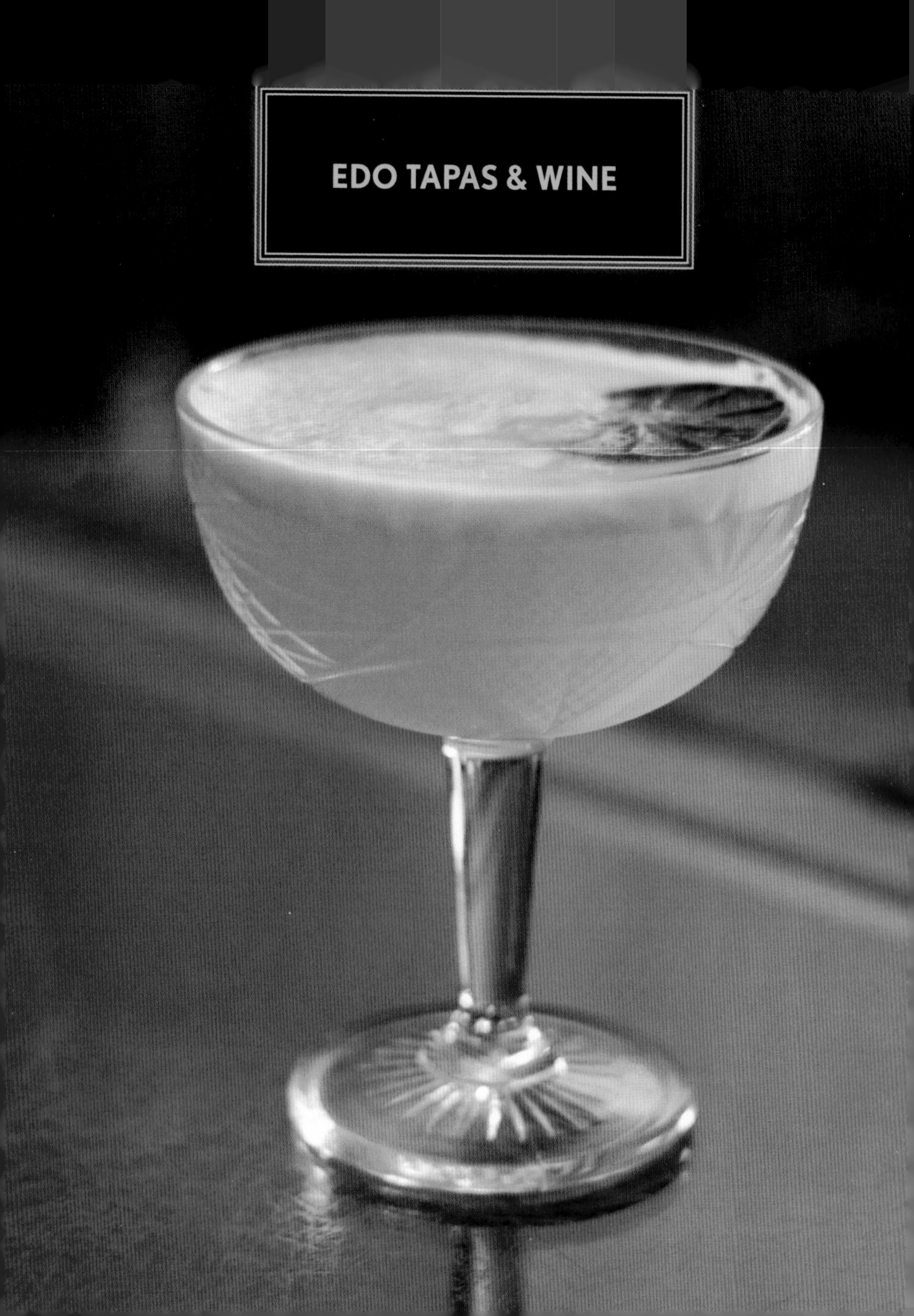

# – CATALUNYA –

As the name suggests, Edo Tapas & Wine is inspired by the Spanish tradition of eating small portions of savory dishes with wine or cocktails. Raised in Barcelona, chef Oscar Amador Edo grew up immersed in the rich cuisine of Catalonia, which is fed by the generous fruits of the Mediterranean.

GLASSWARE: **Coupe**

GARNISH: **Dehydrated lime wheel (see page 166)**

- 1½ oz. Diplomático Planas rum
- ¾ oz. fresh lime juice
- ¾ oz. Honey Syrup
- ¾ oz. aquafaba (see page 300)
- 2 oz. Cava, to top

1. Chill the coupe.

2. Add all of the ingredients, except for the Cava, to a cocktail shaker filled with ice, shake vigorously until chilled, and strain into the chilled coupe.

3. Top with the Cava and garnish with the dehydrated lime wheel.

HONEY SYRUP: Place 1 part honey and 1 part water in a saucepan and bring to a simmer, stirring until the honey has emulsified. Remove from heat and let cool completely before using or storing.

# – EDO GIN & TONIC –

A very simple yet flavorful cocktail. The infused gin and garnishes are what give this drink that extra dimension you're looking for when you order a classic at the bar.

GLASSWARE: **Coupe or wine glass**

GARNISH: **Strip of orange peel, black peppercorn, and sprig of fresh lavender**

• **1½ oz. Infused Sipsmith Gin**      • **3 oz. Q Tonic Water**

1. Add the ingredients to a coupe or wine glass containing a large block of ice and stir until chilled.

2. Express the strip of orange peel over the cocktail and add it as a garnish, alongside a black peppercorn and a sprig of lavender.

INFUSED SIPSMITH GIN: Place a bunch of fresh lavender sprigs, 10 black peppercorns, and 4 halved oranges into a Porthole Infuser, add a 750 ml bottle of gin, and let the mixture steep for at least 24 hours. Strain before using or storing.

## FRANKIE'S TIKI ROOM

Escape from the hustle and bustle of Vegas by following the giant pink neon sign to this 24-hour-a-day fantasyland. Outlandish music, one-of-a-kind tiki mugs, and exotic flavors await.

# – TONGA REEFER –

J ust one hit of this high-octane treat will mellow out even the most stone-faced individual.

GLASSWARE: **Pilsner glass**

GARNISH: **Vanilla bean and (optional) edible flower**

- 1 oz. Cruzan Rum
- ½ oz. Whaler's Vanille Rum
- ½ oz. Wray & Nephew White Overproof Rum

- ½ oz. fresh lime juice
- 2 oz. guava nectar
- ½ oz. Whaler's Original Dark Rum, to top

1. Fill the pilsner glass with ice and add all of the ingredients, except for the dark rum.

2. Pour the contents of the glass into a cocktail shaker, shake vigorously until chilled, and then pour the cocktail back into the glass.

3. Top with dark rum and garnish with a vanilla bean and, should the mood strike you, an edible flower.

# – DEMON RHUMBA –

This high-voltage jolt of orangey goodness will exorcise your demons. But drink two and they will come back twice as strong.

GLASSWARE: **Pilsner glass**

GARNISH: **Fresh mint leaves**

- 1½ oz. Bacardi O (orange-flavored rum)
- ½ oz. Cointreau
- ½ oz. Hana Bay 151 Rum
- ¼ oz. fresh lime juice
- ¼ oz. orange bitters
- 1 oz. Sweet & Sour
- 2 oz. Fanta Orange Soda

1. Add ice to the pilsner glass, add all of the ingredients, and then pour the mixture into a cocktail shaker. Shake vigorously until chilled and then pour the contents of the shaker back into the pilsner glass.

2. Garnish with the mint leaves.

SWEET & SOUR: In a 12 oz. bottle, combine 2 oz. fresh lemon juice, 4 oz. fresh lime juice, and 6 oz. Simple Syrup (see page 15) and shake vigorously until combined. Store in the refrigerator.

# – SCURVY –

**D**oes this brisk bracer cure it or cause it? Drink a couple and you will have the answer to this question, and many others.

GLASSWARE: **Snifter**

GARNISH: **Strip of grapefruit peel and sprig of fresh mint**

- 2 oz. Cruzan Citrus Rum
- 1½ oz. Cruzan Aged Light Rum
- 1 oz. Cruzan Coconut Rum
- 1 dash Angostura Bitters
- 2 oz. pineapple juice
- 2 oz. Sweet & Sour (see page 190)
- ¼ oz. Coco Lopez Cream of Coconut
- 1 dash Simple Syrup (see page 15)
- 5 lime wedges
- 6 fresh mint leaves
- 1 pinch Hawaiian red alaea salt
- 2 oz. club soda, to top
- 2 oz. 7UP, to top

1. Add all of the ingredients to a cocktail shaker, except the club soda and 7UP, and gently muddle.

2. Add ice, shake vigorously until chilled, and strain into a snifter filled with ice.

3. Top with the club soda and 7UP and garnish with a strip of grapefruit peel and a sprig of mint.

## HAMPTONS

The sheer confusion that results when you tell a Vegas local, "I'm going to the Hamptons" is priceless. Do not be confused, we are still in Las Vegas. This stylish indoor/outdoor restaurant is located in Tivoli Village. The cocktails embody a casual, yet sophisticated experience that will appeal to everyone's palate.

# – BIRDS OF PARADISE –

**S**weet, refreshing, and full of body and flavor, Malibu paired with peach schnapps makes you feel as if you've been transported to a tropical island. The splash of Pomegranate Syrup creates the beautiful red color that stimulates your mind's eye.

GLASSWARE: **Snifter**

GARNISH: **Dehydrated pineapple slice
and toasted coconut flakes**

- 1½ oz. Malibu rum
- 1½ oz. peach schnapps
- 4 oz. pineapple juice
- 1 splash Pomegranate Syrup

1. Add all of the ingredients to a cocktail shaker filled with ice, shake vigorously until chilled, and strain into the snifter.

2. Add ice to the cocktail and garnish with a slice of dehydrated pineapple and toasted coconut flakes.

POMEGRANATE SYRUP: Place 1 cup pomegranate juice, 1 cup sugar, and the juice of ½ lemon in a saucepan and warm over medium heat, stirring until the sugar has dissolved. Reduce heat to low and simmer until the mixture has reduced to a thick syrup. Remove from heat and let cool completely before using or storing.

# – HIBISCUS COSMO –

**C**osmos are always a crowd favorite. But forget about having guests over. Drink a few of these alone while binge-watching your favorite TV show or getting a tan by the pool. If there is one thing you should know about this cocktail, it is that the hibiscus flower has a tremendous amount of health benefits, and adds sweetness to reduce the need for sugar. So drink up!

GLASSWARE: **Cocktail glass**

GARNISH: **Lime slice**

- **2 oz. preferred citrus-flavored vodka**
- **1 oz. Cointreau**
- **½ oz. fresh lime juice**
- **½ oz. Hibiscus Syrup**

1. Add all of the ingredients to a cocktail shaker filled with ice, shake vigorously until chilled, and strain into the cocktail glass.

2. Garnish with the slice of lime.

HIBISCUS SYRUP: Place 1 cup water in a saucepan and bring it to a boil. Remove the pan from heat, add 2 tablespoons of loose-leaf hibiscus tea, and let steep for 10 minutes. Strain the tea back into the saucepan, turn the heat to medium, and add 1 cup sugar. Stir until the sugar has dissolved, reduce heat to low, and let the mixture simmer until it is a thick syrup. Remove from heat and let cool completely before using or storing.

# – BLUEBERRY KOMBUCHA MOJITO –

**K**ombucha, an ancient fermented tea, has received a lot of press lately for its health benefits. With good reason. Kombucha contains antioxidants that help kill off harmful bacteria. It is a good source of probiotics, and may reduce heart disease, protect against cancer, and treat chronic health problems. To see what all the hype is about, add a splash to this Mojito.

GLASSWARE: **Pilsner glass**
GARNISH: **Fresh mint leaves**

- **2 oz. Bacardi Superior white rum**
- **3 sprigs of fresh mint**
- **3 blueberries**
- **½ oz. fresh lime juice**
- **½ oz. Simple Syrup (see page 15)**
- **1 splash Humm Blueberry Mint Kombucha, to top**

1. In a mixing glass, muddle the mint and blueberries, then add ice and the remainder of the ingredients, except the kombucha, and stir.

2. Pour mixture into a pilsner glass over ice and top with the kombucha. Garnish with the mint leaves.

# HEARTHSTONE

Hearthstone is a great restaurant to visit if you feel like taking a vacation from your vacation, otherwise known as a break from The Strip. Many locals love this fun spot in the Red Rock Casino for its festive ambience, great menu, and fantastic service.

# – THANK YOU VERY MATCHA –

I f you plan on ordering this at Hearthstone, do yourself a favor and grab a spot out on the patio. And be sure to sample the food.

GLASSWARE: **Stemless copper wine glass or rocks glass**

GARNISH: **Lemon wheel and fresh mint leaves**

- **1½ oz. Bulldog Gin**
- **1 oz. Matcha Agave**
- **½ oz. fresh lemon juice**
- **3 sprigs of fresh mint**
- **2 oz. Champagne, to top**

1. Add all of the ingredinets, except for the Champagne, to a cocktail shaker filled with ice, shake vigorously until chilled, and strain over ice into the chosen glass.

2. Top with the Champagne and garnish with a lemon wheel and mint leaves.

MATCHA AGAVE: Place 2 cups water in a saucepan and bring to a boil. Remove from heat, stir in 4 cups dark agave nectar, and ¼ cup ground matcha, and let steep for 15 minutes. Strain and let cool completely before using or storing.

**HONEY SALT**

# – ELIZABETH'S GIN & TONIC –

What sets this G & T apart from others is Monkey 47's refreshing lavender notes, founder Elizabeth Blau's favorite tonic, and an invigorating mint-and-lime combination.

GLASSWARE: **Collins glass**

GARNISH: **Lime wedge**

- **2 oz. Monkey 47 Schwarzwald Dry Gin**
- **Handful of fresh mint leaves**
- **1 squeeze fresh lime juice**
- **3 oz. Fever-Tree Naturally Light Tonic Water**

1. Add all of the ingredients to a Collins glass filled with ice and stir until chilled.

2. Garnish with the lime wedge.

# – THE MIDNIGHT RAMBLER –

Inspired by Keith Richards and the Rolling Stones song of the same name, chef Kim Canteenwalla's love of bourbon results in a serious cocktail where the beauty is in its simplicity.

**GLASSWARE:** Rocks glass

**GARNISH:** Strip of orange peel and candied ginger

- **2 oz. Bulleit Bourbon**
- **½ oz. honey**
- **2 dashes aromatic bitters**

1. Add all of the ingredients to a rocks glass containing an ice sphere and stir until chilled.

2. Garnish with a strip of orange peel and candied ginger.

Carrots are a fun, and underutilized, cocktail ingredient; they are full of flavor and nutritional value and have a vibrant aesthetic to boot. Add heat plus Kim's favorite tequila and you get a strong, sexy serve.

GLASSWARE: **Rocks glass**

GARNISH: **Lemon wheel and jalapeño pepper slice**

- **Tajín, for the rim**
- **1½ oz. Casamigos Blanco Tequila**
- **1½ oz. fresh carrot juice**
- **¾ oz. fresh lemon juice**
- **1 jalapeño pepper slice**
- **1 oz. agave nectar**

1. Wet half of the rim of the rocks glass and roll it in the Tajín. Fill the glass with ice.

2. Add the remaining ingredients to a cocktail shaker filled with ice, shake vigorously until chilled, and strain into the rocks glass.

3. Garnish with a lemon wheel and an additional slice of jalapeño.

JERUSALEM MEDITERRANEAN CHEF'S TABLE

# – SPIKED LIMONANA –

his Middle Eastern–inspired drink staves off the desert heat thanks to its refreshing blend of lemon and mint.

GLASSWARE: **Highball glasses**

GARNISH: **Sprigs of fresh mint**

- ½ cup fresh lemon juice
- 3 cups ice
- ¼ cup fresh mint leaves
- 4 oz. vodka
- 2 to 4 oz. Simple Syrup (see page 15)

1. Add all of the ingredients, except for the syrup, to a blender and puree until smooth.

2. Depending on how sweet you want the drink to be, add the desired amount of Simple Syrup to the blender and blitz to incorporate.

3. Pour the cocktail into four glasses and garnish each one with a sprig of mint.

LAWRY'S PRIME RIB

# – VEGAS HEART –

The El Corazon Blend is a mix of passion fruit, blood orange, and pomegranate that is available online or in select stores. If you can't track it down, play around with other elements such as guava or orange blossom water until you land on an arrangement you like.

GLASSWARE: **Cocktail glass**

GARNISH: **Lime wheel**

- Tajín, for rim
- 1½ oz. Chinaco Blanco Tequila
- 2 oz. The Perfect Puree El Corazon Blend
- ¼ oz. fresh lime juice
- 1 oz. sour mix (see page 177 for homemade)
- 1 splash 7UP

1. Wet the rim of the cocktail glass and dip it into the Tajín.

2. Add the remaining ingredients to a cocktail shaker filled with ice, shake vigorously until chilled, and strain into the cocktail glass.

3. Garnish with the lime wheel.

LAYLA GRILL

# – ADIOS MOTHER F'ER (OR AMF) –

**H**ookah lounge Layla Grill offers one of the strongest drinks in town, basically tossing a bunch of well booze into one drink. Fear not, however, the flavor is quite tasty, which makes this potent concoction all the more dangerous.

GLASSWARE: **Cocktail glass**

GARNISH: **Strawberry**

- ◆ 1 oz. tequila
- ◆ 1 oz. vodka
- ◆ 1 oz. gin
- ◆ 1 oz. rum
- ◆ 2 oz. sweet & sour mix (see page 190 for homemade)
- ◆ 1 oz. Sprite or 7UP
- ◆ 1 oz. Blue Curaçao

1. Add all of the ingredients to a cocktail glass filled with ice and stir until chilled.

2. Garnish with the strawberry.

## LOCALE

For an off-the-beaten path option, visit Locale for craft cocktails and a traditional Italian meal.

# – BRUNCH IN MILAN –

D on't just limit the Brunch in Milan to the summertime. A cocktail this packed with fresh, juicy fruit is a great option all year long.

**GLASSWARE:** Wine glass

**GARNISH:** Thin strip of orange peel

- 1½ oz. Ketel One Botanical Peach & Orange Blossom vodka
- ¾ oz. Aperol
- ½ oz. Apricot Puree
- 1½ oz. Avissi Prosecco, to top
- 2 oz. club soda, to top

1. Add the vodka, Aperol, and puree to a cocktail shaker filled with ice and gently shake for just a few seconds.

2. Strain into a wine glass and top with the Prosecco and club soda.

3. Carefully add ice to the glass.

4. Express the strip of orange peel over the cocktail and add it to the drink as a garnish.

**APRICOT PUREE:** Bring a large pot of water to a boil. Fill a bowl with ice water. When the water is boiling, add 2 lbs. ripe apricots, cook for 20 seconds, and then transfer the apricots to the bowl of ice water. Let cool for a few minutes before draining and removing their skins. Halve the apricots and remove the pits. Place the apricots and 3 tablespoons sugar in a saucepan and simmer for 15 minutes, stirring often, until the apricots have broken down into a thick puree. Remove pan from heat and let cool completely before using or storing.

# MARRAKESH

This is a fun place to take a group of visiting friends for a night out. Expect to eat like a true Moroccan: sitting in a tent, enjoying a six-course meal while belly dancers encircle you. Great food, lots of entertainment, and amazing service. What more can you ask for on a trip to Sin City?

# – MANGO MARTINI –

f you've ever wondered what it would be like to live in Marrakesh, sip on one of these cocktails. The orange added by the triple sec really makes this Martini pop.

GLASSWARE: **Cocktail glass**

GARNISH: **Chunk of mango**

- **1 oz. vodka**
- **1 oz. triple sec**
- **2 oz. mango puree or mango juice**
- **½ oz. fresh lime juice**
- **⅓ oz. Simple Syrup (see page 15)**

1. Add all of the ingredients to a cocktail shaker filled with crushed ice, shake vigorously until chilled, and strain into a cocktail glass filled with crushed ice.

2. Garnish with the chunk of mango.

NO REGRETS

# – UNICORNS & SUNSHINE –

The name should be enough to make you stop what you're doing and make this recipe. It has the prettiest combination of colors and the build is so easy. The twist lollipop is not necessary, but it definitely lends a fun touch.

GLASSWARE: **Collins glass**

GARNISH: **Twist lollipop**

- Tajín, for the rim
- 2 oz. Amoretti Premium Passion Fruit Martini Mix
- 2 oz. Fever-Tree Elderflower

Tonic Water
- 1½ oz. Empress 1908 Indigo Gin

1. Wet the rim of the Collins glass and dip it into the Tajín.

2. Fill the Collins glass with ice, add the remaining ingredients in the order they are listed, and stir until chilled.

3. Garnish with the twist lollipop.

# – BREAK THE RULES –

**A**Break the Rules is the perfect creamy cocktail for any vegan friends that might stop by. The combination of the Nevada-based Ambros Banana Whiskey, cold-brew coffee, and the nutty notes of both the orgeat and almond milk makes for a satisfying jolt.

GLASSWARE: **Collins glass**

GARNISH: **Dash of cinnamon**

- 1½ oz. Ambros Banana Whiskey
- ½ oz. Liquid Alchemist Orgeat
- 2 oz. cold-brew coffee
- 2 oz. unsweetened almond milk

1. Add all of the ingredients to a mixing glass filled with ice, stir until chilled, and strain into a Collins glass filled with ice.

2. Gently stir the cocktail and garnish with the dash of cinnamon.

# – MILKY WAY MARTINI –

T he Milky Way Martini is one of No Regrets' signature drinks, and
for good reason. This fun dessert drink is decadent and delicious.

GLASSWARE: **Cocktail glass**

GARNISH: **Chocolate syrup and caramel syrup**

- 1½ oz. Skyy Infusions Vanilla
  Bean Vodka
- ½ oz. Godiva White
  Chocolate liqueur
- ½ oz. Godiva Chocolate
  liqueur
- ½ oz. half & half
- 1 drizzle caramel syrup

1. Add all of the ingredients to a cocktail shaker filled with ice, shake
vigorously until chilled, and strain into the cocktail glass.

2. Garnish with the chocolate and caramel syrups.

PIERO'S

# – SPARK PLUG –

A shooter with a kick, thanks to the espresso.

GLASSWARE: **Shot glass**

GARNISH: **None**

- **2 parts vanilla-flavored vodka**
- **1 part vodka**
- **1 part brewed espresso**
- **1 part Kahlùa**

1. Add all of the ingredients to a cocktail shaker filled with ice, shake vigorously until chilled, and strain into the shot glass.

# – MONKEY'S AVIATION –

**D**own a couple of these delicious, potent cocktails and you'll find out what would happen if you let a monkey fly a plane.

GLASSWARE: **Coupe**

GARNISH: **Maraschino cherry and orange slice**

- **2 oz. Monkey 47 Schwarzwald Dry Gin**
- **¼ oz. crème de violette**
- **½ oz. maraschino cherry liqueur**
- **¾ oz. fresh lemon juice**

1. Add all of the ingredients to a cocktail shaker filled with ice, shake vigorously until chilled, and strain into the coupe.

2. Garnish with a maraschino cherry and an orange slice.

# – VGK PUCK DROP –

The black sugar rim is meant to evoke a hockey puck. Go, Golden Knights, go!

GLASSWARE: **Cocktail glass**

GARNISH: **None**

- **Black sugar, for the rim**
- **3 oz. lemon-flavored vodka**
- **2 oz. sour mix (see page 177 for homemade)**
- **1 oz. limoncello**

1. Wet the rim of the cocktail glass and dip it into the black sugar.

2. Add the remaining ingredients to a cocktail shaker filled with ice, shake vigorously until chilled, and strain into the cocktail glass.

# – CAMPFIRE S'MORES –

This wouldn't be a PKWY Tavern recipe if it didn't include beer. Thank mixologist Mark Hefter for creating the perfect drink to sip while sitting by a campfire in winter.

**GLASSWARE: Pint glass**

**GARNISH: Toasted marshmallow**

- Graham cracker crumbs, for the rim
- Chocolate shavings, for the rim
- 1½ oz. Bulleit Bourbon
- 1½ oz. Giffard Crème de Cacao (white)
- 12 oz. Garage Brewing Co. Marshmallow Milk Stout, to top

1. Place the graham cracker crumbs and chocolate shavings in a dish and stir to combine. Wet the rim of the pint glass and dip it into the mixture.

2. Add the bourbon and crème de cacao to a cocktail shaker filled with ice, shake vigorously until chilled, and strain into the pint glass.

3. Top with the stout and garnish with the toasted marshmallow.

WEERA THAI

# − BUTTERFLY BITTER −

A sweet, beautiful cocktail that helps balance out some of the spice in the food turned out by this authentic Thai restaurant, which, unfortunately, is no longer a secret only the locals are in on.

- 2 oz. soju
- 2 oz. passion fruit wine
- 1 oz. lychee nectar
- ¼ oz. Monin Lychee Syrup
- ½ oz. fresh lime juice
- ½ oz. b'lure Butterfly Pea Flower Extract, to top

1. Add all of the ingredients, except for the pea flower extract, to a cocktail shaker filled with ice, shake vigorously until chilled, and strain into the cocktail glass.

2. Layer the pea flower extract on top of the cocktail.

3. Garnish with the rose petal.

# THE SAND DOLLAR LOUNGE

Sitting at the gateway to Las Vegas' booming Chinatown, The Sand Dollar Lounge is a local landmark enjoying the rush of being granted a new lease on life. Originally opened as a blues bar in 1976, over its first 30 years The Sand Dollar became a draw for iconic musicians including Muddy Waters, B. B. King, and even Mick Jagger. Hit by hard times, the bar closed its doors in 2007, but its spirit was restless. Within two years it was purchased and reignited by a team of hospitality veterans: Anthony Jamison, Benito Martinez, and Nathan Grates. Honoring the tradition and history of the iconic venue, The Sand Dollar Lounge has reclaimed its beloved spot as a premier live music venue, featuring free entertainment nightly.

# – SINK THE PINK –

T he song by AC/DC inspired this perfectly balanced cocktail. The deceptively simple garnish works wonders on the aroma. Focus on expressing the oils from the lemon peel onto the rim of the glass, rather than into the drink.

GLASSWARE: **Coupe**

GARNISH: **Strip of lemon peel**

- **6 pink peppercorns**
- **1½ oz. Whistling Andy Pink Peppercorn Pear Gin**
- **½ oz. Aperol**
- **1 oz. fresh lemon juice**
- **½ oz. Simple Syrup (see page 15)**
- **2 dashes Peychaud's Bitters**

1. Add the pink peppercorns to a cocktail shaker and muddle.

2. Add ice and the remaining ingredients, shake vigorously until chilled, and double-strain into the coupe.

3. Express the lemon peel's oils by rubbing it against the rim of the glass. Then affix it to the rim as a garnish—do not drop it in the drink.

A classic drink created by mixologist Chase Gordon, inspired by the Tame Impala hit.

- 1½ oz. Cimarrón Reposado Tequila
- ¾ oz. Rapa Giovanni Amaro
- ½ oz. Amaro Averna
- 2 dashes Fee Brothers Old Fashioned Bitters

1. Add all of the ingredients to a mixing glass filled with ice, stir until chilled, and strain over ice into the coupe.

2. Garnish with the tattooed orange peel.

TATTOOED ORANGE PEEL: Simply use a serrated knife to score a strip of orange peel with a design of your choosing.

# – F*CK THE PAIN AWAY –

This drink shares its name with the notorious Peaches's song. The peach and ginger beer say summer, but the pear and absinthe say autumn. Which really means this is a perfect cocktail any time of year, especially in the desert, where the seasons change subtly.

GLASSWARE: **Collins glass**

GARNISH: **Dehydrated Peach Slice**

- **1½ oz. Ketel One Peach & Orange Blossom**
- **1 oz. St. George Spiced Pear liqueur**
- **¼ oz. absinthe**
- **3 oz. ginger beer**

1. Add all of the ingredients to a Collins glass filled with ice and gently stir until chilled.

2. Garnish with the Dehydrated Peach Slice.

DEHYDRATED PEACH SLICE: Cut 1 peach into thin slices and arrange the slices on a piece of parchment paper; insert into a dehydrator set at 120°F and leave for 12 hours.

# – ELEPHANT IN THE ROOM –

The Elephant in the Room is the Sparrow + Wolf's twist on the classic Mint Julep. Alyssa Ocampo, one of the lead bartenders, was looking to create a cocktail with a flavor profile that evoked the summer and landed on a combination of mint and watermelon. Ocampo says that the early iteration of this drink was way too sweet and was advised to add lemon or lime juice. However, that would mean the cocktail would be shaken and not stirred, which is not the traditional method for making a Mint Julep. Instead, she threw in some pickled watermelon rinds along with a housemade pickle brine, which ultimately worked perfectly.

GLASSWARE: **Elephant mug or rocks glass**
GARNISH: **Sprig of fresh mint, cube of pickled watermelon rind, and pinch of ground coriander or cardamom**

- ½ oz. mint syrup
- ¾ oz. pickle brine
- 2 oz. Watermelon-Infused Ophir Gin*

1. Add all of the ingredients to a mixing glass, stir until chilled, and strain over crushed ice into the chosen glass.

2. Garnish with a sprig of mint, a cube of pickled watermelon rind, and sprinkle of the chosen ground spice.

*Ophir Gin is an Indian gin distinguished by the notes of coriander and cardamom.*

# – DON'T CRY WOLF –

The bartenders took ingredients that were coming from the kitchen and played around until they found the perfect version of a Margarita. Smoke is very prominent in many of Sparrow + Wolf's dishes, so they decided to add just a touch of an infused mezcal to this cocktail. The Sichuan Foam is really the shining star in this cocktail, however. What looks like whipped cream is actually an egg white-based foam that is infused with a Sichuan tincture and syrup, adding a layer of floral notes to the cocktail and leaving your tongue slightly abuzz. The cocktail is then dusted with Chive Dust, which adds a layer of umami to the drink.

GLASSWARE: **Rocks glass**

GARNISH: **Dehydrated citrus wheel (see page 166)**

- 1½ oz. Espolòn Tequila
- ½ oz. Thai Chili Mezcal
- ½ oz. agave nectar
- ½ oz. fresh lime juice
- ½ oz. fresh lemon juice
- Sichuan Foam, to top
- 1 sprinkle Chive Dust

1. Add all of the ingredients, except for the foam and chive dust, to a cocktail shaker filled with ice, shake vigorously until chilled, and strain into a rocks glass.

2. Fill the glass with ice, top with the Sichuan Foam, and sprinkle the chive dust on top.

3. Garnish with the dehydrated citrus wheel.

**THAI CHILI MEZCAL:** Combine 1 bottle of mezcal with sliced Thai chili (amount depends on your spice threshold) in a glass jar. The longer it sits the spicier it will get so no matter how many peppers are used, taste every 24 hours. Once desired flavor is achieved strain and store.

**SICHUAN FOAM:** To make this foam, first make Sichuan Syrup. In a saucepan over medium heat combine 2½ cups sugar with 2½ cups water and stir until sugar is dissolved. Remove pan from heat, add 1 oz. Sichuan peppercorns, and let steep for 20 minutes. Strain and store. Next, make the Sichuan Tincture by combining 2½ cups vodka with 1 oz. Sichuan peppercorns in a glass jar and letting it sit for at least 3 days before straining and storing. When ready to make Sichuan Foam, combine 5½ oz. egg whites, 1 oz. Sichuan Tincture, 3 oz. Sichuan Syrup, and ¼ oz. fresh lime juice in a bowl. Emulsify the mixture using a hand blender, then pour into a canister and charge with $CO_2$ 3 times.

**CHIVE DUST:** Leave 1 bunch of fresh chives in dehydrator overnight. The next day run the chives through a spice grinder.

# – SCROOGE McDUCK –

The Scrooge McDuck, a singular take on the Manhattan, is rich and viscous, boozy and bittersweet. The foie gras beefs up the oily texture of the rye without being too heavy, while the grape nectar and simple syrup act as the sweet vermouth. Ocampo had been wanting to experiment with fat-washing, but never got around to it because she thought the process was too time-consuming. Turns out, it's extremely simple! Since foie gras is served daily at Sparrow + Wolf, Ocampo asked the kitchen to render off the fat for her. Just as Scrooge McDuck swims in his gold, here we have gold swimming in duck.

GLASSWARE: **Coupe**

GARNISH: **Gold-painted nasturtium leaf**

- **2 oz. Foie Gras–Washed High West Double Rye**
- **¼ oz. Domaine Santé Grape Nectar**
- **¼ oz. Simple Syrup (see page 15)**
- **4 dashes lemon bitters**

1. Add all of the ingredients to a mixing glass filled with ice, stir until chilled, and strain into the coupe.

2. Garnish with a gold-painted nasturtium leaf.

**FOIE GRAS-WASHED HIGH WEST DOUBLE RYE (ADJUST QUANTITIES AS NEEDED):** Add a 750 ml bottle of High West Double Rye into a nonreactive container; add 1½ oz. rendered foie gras fat to the whiskey, give it a good stir, and let sit at room temperature for 1 hour. Place whiskey in freezer overnight. The fat will solidify in a layer at the top. Remove the fat layer and strain the whiskey through a coffee filter before using or storing.

PARTAGE

# – GOURMET LEMON –

This drink doubles as a dessert, thanks to the torched meringue floating on top.

GLASSWARE: **Coupe**

GARNISH: **Sprig of fresh mint and dehydrated lemon wheel (see page 166)**

- • **1½ oz. silver tequila**
- • **¾ oz. limoncello**
- • **¾ oz. fresh lime juice**

- • **2 dashes lemon bitters**
- • **Meringue, to top**

1. Add all of the ingredients, other than the Meringue, to a mixing glass filled with ice, stir until chilled, and strain into the coupe.

2. Top with the Meringue and torch until it is browned.

3. Garnish with a sprig of mint and a dehydrated lemon wheel.

MERINGUE (ADJUST QUANTITIES AS NEEDED): Whip 4 large, room-temperature egg whites until they are glossy and begin to form peaks. Add ¼ teaspoon cream of tartar to the egg whites and then slowly beat in ¼ cup of sugar. Beat until the mixture is smooth and can hold stiff peaks.

# THE GOLDEN TIKI

Take a voyage through a lava rock cave to enter this hidden gem in Chinatown, which is decorated with all the tiki trappings, including skull racks, a giant conch shell, and cargo cult artifacts. A long-time "cocktailian," member of the Health & Wellness Committee for the United States Bartenders Guild in Las Vegas, and lead bartender at The Golden Tiki, Adam Rains has a true passion for food and drink. His drive has inspired him to keep apace with all the latest trends and developments in the industry. His mantra with both food and cocktails: "French is best."

# – BLUE MARINER –

This exotic, refreshing, and flavorful Golden Tiki treasure is fun to drink, pairing perfectly with the lounge's casually gilded vibe.

**GLASSWARE:** Large snifter
**GARNISH:** Flaming Lime Shell, pineapple leaves, and edible flowers

- 1½ oz. Wray & Nephew Overproof Rum
- 1 oz. Blue Mariner Curaçao
- 1 oz. pineapple juice
- 1 oz. fresh lime juice

1. Add all of the ingredients to a cocktail shaker containing 1 or 2 ice cubes and vigorously "whip shake" the cocktail.

2. Strain into a large snifter filled with crushed ice.

3. Garnish with a Flaming Lime Shell, pineapple leaves, and edible flowers.

**BLUE MARINER CURAÇAO:** Combine 4 parts Grand Mariner, 4 parts Simple Syrup (see page 15), 1 part Green Chartreuse, and ½ part blue food coloring.

**FLAMING LIME SHELL:** Use a citrus squeezer to remove the pulp from a lime half and mold the shell back into shape, smoothing out any fruit fiber. This is your vessel. Place a sugar cube or crouton soaked in overproof rum or lemon extract in the center to serve as the wick. If you're looking to extend the show, use lemon extract because it will remain alight a bit longer than rum will. Float the citrus shell in the drink and light the cube. When the flame burns out—bottoms up!

# DOWNTOWN

STRAWBERRY FIELDS • HUNTER S. MASH • LITTLE
HOT MESS • LONDON COMMONS • PADDINGTON •
STIEGL BEAGLE • BE COOL-ADA • CIRCE'S KISS •
LAVENDER LOVER • SCOTCH 80S • THE KINGSMAN •
MAC 'N' SLOSH • ALL THE FEELS • PEPPERONI PIZZA
BLOODY MARY • POST MELON • THE MOREY •
RHUBARB REFRESHER • MELLOW HIGH • MULE
SUGAR • APPLE PIE HARVEST • RED LIGHT DISTRICT •
CONSIGLIERE • Q 1908 • MOONSHINE MAYHEM • THE
MARLOW • THE SMASH • BLOOD OF MY ENEMIES •
POP'S SECRET

**P**rior to The Strip dominating the minds of millions, Downtown was the gambling district in Las Vegas. Fremont Street, which is named after American explorer John C. Frémont (who was also the first presidential candidate from the Republican Party), is considered one of the most famous streets in the Valley besides The Strip. It was the first paved street in Las Vegas, and it also hosts millions of visitors a year.

ATOMIC LIQUORS

# – STRAWBERRY FIELDS –

**A**tomic Liquors, the oldest freestanding bar in Las Vegas, boasts the city's first package liquor license and off-sales permit. In its heyday, this bar, which was named for its customers' fondness for watching atomic blasts from the roof, counted the Rat Pack, Smothers Brothers, Clint Eastwood, and Barbra Streisand among its regulars.

GLASSWARE: **Rocks glass**

GARNISH: **Strawberry**

- 1¼ oz. gin
- ¾ oz. strawberry syrup
- ½ oz. Campari
- ½ oz. St-Germain
- ¾ oz. fresh lemon juice
- ¼ oz. Basil Shrub

1. Add all of the ingredients to a cocktail shaker filled with ice, shake vigorously until chilled, and strain over ice into a rocks glass.

2. Garnish with the strawberry.

BASIL SHRUB: Place 2 cups sugar and 3 quarts white balsamic vinegar in a saucepan and cook over medium heat, stirring frequently until the sugar has dissolved. Add 2 cups fresh basil leaves and gently simmer for 20 minutes; do not let the basil turn brown. Remove from heat and let cool completely. Strain before using or storing.

# – HUNTER S. MASH –

**W**hen the owners of Atomic Liquors were cleaning out the back rooms, they found bottles of Old Crow Whiskey from 1976. After some research, they discovered that Old Crow was Hunter S. Thompson's favorite spirit. And so the Hunter S. Mash, the bar's best-selling cocktail, was created.

GLASSWARE: **Collins glass**

GARNISH: **Sprig of fresh mint**

- **5 fresh mint leaves**
- **1½ oz. Old Crow Whiskey**
- **½ oz. Aperol**
- **¾ oz. fresh lemon juice**
- **¾ oz. Ginger Syrup (see page 50)**
- **2 oz. club soda**

1. Place the mint in the Collins glass and muddle. Add all of the remaining ingredients, except for the club soda, in the order they are listed (i.e., build the cocktail in the glass), add ice, and stir until chilled.

2. Top with the club soda and garnish with the sprig of mint.

# COMMONWEALTH

This stylish, 6,000-square-foot bar sits on the very busy corner of Fremont Street and South 6th Street, and has become a popular spot for locals, many of whom wish it were still Downtown's best kept secret. If you are a fan of art related to the Prohibition era, this is the venue for you. If you're lucky, you'll find their secret bar, which is hidden behind one of the many doors. To enter, you will need to find the number to text for a reservation. Otherwise, make your way upstairs to the rooftop bar for a fun view, upbeat music, and more art.

# – LITTLE HOT MESS –

The combination of the Bacardi Dragon Berry, strawberry, and lime juice make for a bold, creative drink.

GLASSWARE: **Rocks glass**
GARNISH: **Lime wedge and strawberry slice**

- **3 strawberries**
- **1½ oz. Bacardi Dragon Berry Rum**
- **1 oz. fresh lime juice**
- **1 oz. Simple Syrup (see page 15)**
- **Club soda, to top**

1. Place the strawberries in a cocktail shaker and muddle.

2. Add the remaining ingredients, except for the club soda, to the cocktail shaker, add ice, shake vigorously until chilled, and strain over ice into a rocks glass.

3. Top with the club soda and garnish with a lime wedge and a slice of strawberry.

# – LONDON COMMONS –

I f you like a classic Gin & Tonic, you'll love this slightly sweeter, more refreshing twist.

GLASSWARE: **Rocks glass**

GARNISH: **Lime wedge and cucumber slice**

- 3 cucumber slices
- 1½ oz. Hendrick's Gin
- 1 oz. fresh lime juice
- 1 oz. Simple Syrup (see page 15)
- Club soda, to top

1. Place the cucumber slices in a cocktail shaker and muddle.

2. Add the rest of the ingredients, except for the club soda, to the cocktail shaker, add ice, shake vigorously until chilled, and strain over ice into a rocks glass.

3. Top with the club soda and garnish with a lime wedge and an additional slice of cucumber.

# – PADDINGTON –

A very simple, yet delicious cocktail that is easy to make at home if you can't get to Commonwealth.

GLASSWARE: **Cocktail glass**

GARNISH: **None**

- 1½ oz. rye whiskey
- 1 oz. sweet vermouth
- ½ oz. triple sec
- 2 dashes orange bitters
- 2 dashes chocolate bitters

1. Add all of the ingredients to a mixing glass filled with ice, stir until chilled, and strain into the cocktail glass.

# REBAR

ReBAR is the only bar in the world where "Everything's for sale," with proceeds from purchased knickknacks and food and drink specials getting donated to local charities. Owner Derek Stonebarger says that for the right price, he'll even sell you the bar. All jokes aside, purchasing a cocktail at ReBAR means you are giving back to the community.

# – STIEGL BEAGLE –

**B**uy this cocktail at ReBAR and help support Forget Me Not Animal Sanctuary, a nonprofit, no-kill organization dedicated to rescuing animals that have been abandoned.

GLASSWARE: **Collins glass**

GARNISH: **Lime wheel**

- Salt, for the rim
- 1 squeeze fresh lime juice
- 1½ oz. El Toro Silver Tequila
- 4 oz. Stiegl Radler Grapefruit

1. Wet the rim of the Collins glass and dip it into the salt.

2. Fill the glass with ice, add the lime juice, and then simultaneously pour in the tequila and beer until the glass is full.

3. Garnish with the lime wheel.

# – BE COOL-ADA –

**D**avy's, right next door to ReBAR, is run by the same folks and also has a philanthropic bent. The Be Cool-Ada, a fun twist on a Piña Colada, is one of the charitable cocktails, with a portion of proceeds going to the Cupcake Girls Charity, a confidential support system for those involved in the sex industry.

GLASSWARE: **Rocks glass**

GARNISH: **Maraschino cherry**

- 1½ oz. Papa's Pilar Blonde Rum
- ¾ oz. fresh lime juice
- ¾ oz. Reàl Cream of Coconut
- Pineapple juice, to top

1. Add the rum, lime juice, and cream of coconut to a cocktail shaker filled with ice, shake for about 5 seconds, and strain over ice into a rocks glass.

2. Fill the rest of the glass with pineapple juice, give the drink a good stir, and garnish with the maraschino cherry.

## DOWNTOWN COCKTAIL ROOM

Located in the heart of Vegas, this speakeasy-style bar was established by Michael Cornthwaite in 2007. Don't be surprised when you can't find this place. It's called a speakeasy for a reason. The location is discreet, with a hidden entrance on Las Vegas Boulevard.

# — CIRCE'S KISS —

**F**loral, herbaceous, and slightly sweet, this mystical and botanical potion is sure to put you under its enchanting spell.

GLASSWARE: **Coupe**

GARNISH: **Chamomile flowers and ground freeze-dried raspberries**

- 1½ oz. gin
- ¼ oz. absinthe
- ¾ oz. Chamomile Syrup
- 1 oz. coconut milk
- ½ oz. aquafaba (see page 300)

1. Add all of the ingredients to a cocktail shaker filled with ice, shake vigorously until chilled, and strain into the coupe.

2. Garnish with chamomile flowers and ground freeze-dried raspberries, which should be sprinkled on top of the foam in the shape of a crescent moon.

CHAMOMILE SYRUP: Add 1 tablespoon of chamomile flowers or 2 bags of chamomile tea to a standard Simple Syrup (see page 15) after the sugar has dissolved. Let cool and strain before using or storing.

# – LAVENDER LOVER –

Lavender and mint delicately tease your nose before tap dancing on your tongue.

GLASSWARE: **Wine glass**

GARNISH: **Sprig of fresh mint**

- **Absinthe, to rinse**
- **10 fresh mint leaves**
- **½ oz. Simple Syrup (see page 15)**
- **2 oz. Lavender-Infused Gin**
- **¾ oz. crème de violette**
- **¾ oz. fresh lemon juice**
- **Club soda, to top**

1. Rinse the wine glass with the absinthe.

2. Place the mint and simple syrup in a cocktail shaker and muddle. Add ice and the gin, crème de violette, and lemon juice and shake vigorously until chilled.

3. Strain the cocktail into the wine glass, top with the club soda, and garnish with the sprig of mint.

LAVENDER-INFUSED GIN: Add 10 dried lavender buds to a 750 ml bottle of gin and steep for 24 hours. Strain before using or storing.

# – SCOTCH 80s –

**B**oozy, ambrosial, lively, and, like its namesake, hip!

GLASSWARE: **Rocks glass**

GARNISH: **Slice of strawberry**

- 1½ oz. Canadian whisky
- ½ oz. Scotch
- ½ oz. sweet vermouth
- ¼ oz. Bénédictine

1. Build the cocktail in a rocks glass filled with ice, stir until chilled, and garnish with the slice of strawberry.

# ESTHER'S KITCHEN

Born and raised in Las Vegas, James Trees's culinary career has been defined by an impressive drive to learn. While still a student at Las Vegas High School, he joined the kitchen team at the then-cutting edge Mirage Hotel & Casino. Trees spent two years under chef Luke Palladino prior to beginning formal training at The Culinary Institute of America in Hyde Park, New York. At 21, he returned to The Strip as the youngest sous chef ever hired at the five-star, four-diamond Bellagio Hotel & Casino, working for Michael Mina's Aqua. He then joined the kitchen at Bradley Ogden in Caesars Palace (Best New Restaurant award from the James Beard Foundation, a first for any Las Vegas restaurant), then (interrupted briefly by a near-fatal auto accident) returned to the Mina team as corporate sous chef and opened five new restaurants with that team, including XIV with Steven Fretz.

After a year working behind the scenes on Gordon Ramsay's *Kitchen Nightmares,* Trees played a vital role in the culinary revival of Los Angeles, with positions including chef de cuisine at FIG under Ray Garcia, and corporate chef for Superba Bread and Pitfire Artisan Pizza. Other experiences along the way included time with Eric Ripert and Akasha Richmond, and a stint at Britain's legendary The Fat Duck.

After scaling some of the most impressive heights in the restaurant business, no ambition was calling Trees more than bringing it all back home. Esther's Kitchen, named for the great aunt who served as Trees's first mentor, is the ideal local restaurant: drawing inspiration from its neighborhood—the arts district—elevating the simple, and simplifying the elegant.

Grounded in the ingredient-driven cuisine of Italy, the pastas, breads, and nearly everything else at Esther's is made in-house; produce and proteins come from the best local sources available; wines are chosen for intrigue and value; cocktails are mixed to please the customer, not a bartender's ego. All in all, Esther's is a restaurant you'll quickly want to call home.

# – THE KINGSMAN –

**W**hat do you get when you combine chocolate-covered bacon, orange, and rye whiskey? A rich, robust, autumn-inflected cocktail.

**GLASSWARE:** **Rocks glass**

**GARNISH:** **Slice of Rye Candy-and-Chocolate Covered Bacon**

- 1½ oz. Lip Service Rye Whiskey
- ½ oz. Bigallet China-China liqueur
- ½ oz. The Bitter Truth EXR Amaro
- ¼ oz. bourbon barrel-aged maple syrup
- 2 dashes chocolate bitters
- 4 dashes Bittercube Corazon Bitters

1. Add all of the ingredients to a mixing glass filled with ice, stir until chilled, and strain into a rocks glass containing a large block of ice.

2. Garnish with the slice of Rye Candy-and-Chocolate Covered Bacon.

**RYE CANDY-AND-CHOCOLATE COVERED BACON:** Sprinkle the zest of 6 oranges onto a parchment-lined baking sheet. Set the oven to the lowest temperature possible, place the zest in the oven, and roast the orange zest until it has dried out to the desired level. Remove from the oven and raise the oven's temperature to 400°F. Place slices of bacon on a parchment-lined baking sheet and bake for 20 minutes, or until crisp. Remove the bacon from the oven, let it cool, and reduce the oven's temperature to 350°F. Bring 1 inch of water to boil in a saucepan, add

1 part Lip Service Rye and 2 parts sugar to a heatproof mixing bowl, and place the bowl over the saucepan. Stir until the sugar has dissolved and then dip the slices of bacon into the mixture. Place the coated bacon on a wire rack set into a parchment-lined baking sheet. Bake the glazed bacon at 350°F for about 15 minutes. Remove from the oven and let cool. Place milk chocolate in a microwave-safe bowl and microwave on medium until melted, removing to stir every 15 seconds. Dip half of each slice of bacon into the melted chocolate, place it back on the wire rack, and sprinkle with sea salt and the roasted orange zest.

# – MAC 'N' SLOSH –

A cocktail for the apple pie lover. However strong your love may be, remember to sip, not chug, this drink.

GLASSWARE: **Rocks glass**

GARNISH: **Apple slices and Cinnamon Sugar**

- 1½ oz. Malahat Spiced Rum
- ½ oz. fresh lemon juice
- 1 oz. fresh-pressed honeycrisp apple juice
- ½ oz. Cinnamon Syrup
- 4 dashes Peychaud's Bitters, to float

1. Add all of the ingredients, except for the bitters, to a cocktail shaker filled with ice, shake vigorously until chilled, and strain into a rocks glass containing a large block of ice.

2. Float the bitters on top of the cocktail and garnish with apple slices and a line of Cinnamon Sugar.

CINNAMON SUGAR: Combine 2 parts cinnamon with 1 part sugar.

CINNAMON SYRUP: Add 3 cinnamon sticks to a standard Simple Syrup (see page 15) after the sugar has dissolved. Remove from heat, let cool, and remove the cinnamon sticks before using or storing.

# — ALL THE FEELS —

ndulge in a cocktail blend that truly evokes a swirl of emotions.

**GLASSWARE:** Collins glass

**GARNISH:** Strip of lemon peel, slice of strawberry,
and sprig of fresh dill

- 1½ oz. Strawberry-Infused Tequila
- ½ oz. Dolin Blanc
- ½ oz. Casoni 1814 Aperitivo
- ½ oz. Rhubarb Syrup
- ¾ oz. fresh lemon juice
- 1 dash celery bitters
- 1 splash soda water
- Prosecco, to top

**1.** Add all of the ingredients, except for the soda water and Prosecco, to a cocktail shaker filled with ice and shake vigorously until chilled.

**2.** Add the soda water to a Collins glass filled with ice, strain the cocktail into the glass, and top with the Prosecco. Garnish with a strip of lemon peel, a slice of strawberry, and a sprig of dill.

**STRAWBERRY-INFUSED TEQUILA:** Place 1 cup chopped strawberries and a 750 ml bottle of tequila in a mason jar and let steep for 48 hours. Strain before using or storing.

**RHUBARB SYRUP:** Add 1 cup chopped rhubarb to a standard Simple Syrup (see page 15) after the sugar has dissolved. Simmer for 10 minutes, remove from heat, and let cool completely. Strain before using or storing.

# SPOTLIGHT: KEITH BRACEWELL

A native of Houston, Texas, Keith Bracewell believes in balance in all aspects of his life and career. Splitting his creative energies between the worlds of music and mixology, Bracewell first rose to prominence at Houston hotspots Dirt Bar and Pub Fiction, where he tended bar while taking time off from playing in touring rock bands. After moving to Los Angeles at age 25, he held management and bar lead positions at Darren's, Jiraffe, and the Sunset Strip House of Blues before combining his two passions at Kiss' first Rock & Brews location. Next, Bracewell headed north to San Francisco, where he spent time at more craft-oriented bars like Rx and The Douglas Room. After that, Sonia Stelea tapped him to join her at Esther's Kitchen in Las Vegas.

Bracewell is now bar manager at Esther's, where he leads an impressive team of award-winning mix masters. He favors seasonal ingredients, and his go-to spirit is anything agave-based.

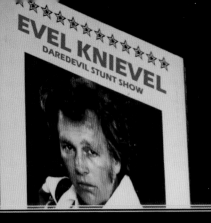

## EVEL PIE

No, the name isn't a typo. There's only one way to spell the "Evel" in Evel Knievel, the patron saint of this pizza joint with an edge, and lots of daredevil memorabilia. And pies with funny, catchy names. During the Vegas grasshopper infestation (look up the videos) Evel Pie created a grasshopper pizza, using the traditional Mexican ingredient of dried grasshoppers. Branden Powers, managing partner and creator of Evel Pie and The Golden Tiki, is serious about not taking anything too seriously, as can be seen in these eclectic cocktails.

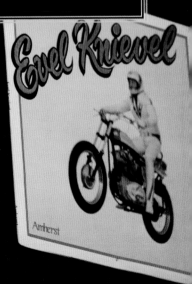

# – PEPPERONI PIZZA BLOODY MARY –

Created by Trevor Rue, this is Downtown's Bloody Mary! It is full of flavor and a perfect summertime drink when walking around in the morning.

**GLASSWARE:** Pint glass

**GARNISH:** Green olive, slice of banana pepper, and pepperoni

- 2 oz. vodka
- 3½ oz. tomato juice (or lightly seasoned Bloody Mary mix)
- ½ oz. marinara sauce
- ½ oz. pepperoncini brine
- 3 dashes Tabasco
- 3 dashes black pepper
- 2 dashes Worcestershire sauce
- 2 dashes salt
- 1 dash olive brine
- 1 dash A-1
- 2 olives
- 2 pepperoni slices
- 1 squeeze fresh lemon juice
- 1 squeeze fresh lime juice
- Parmesan cheese, grated, to top

1. Add all of the ingredients, except for the Parmesan cheese, to a mixing glass filled with ice. Using another mixing glass, use the Cuban roll method (see page 109) to combine the cocktail. Pour the cocktail and the ice into a pint glass.

2. Sprinkle the Parmesan on top and garnish with a green olive, slice of banana pepper, and pepperoni skewered on a cocktail pick.

# – POST MELON –

T he annual Life Is Beautiful Festival is a big occasion in Vegas, and Rob Lawrence's Post Melon was fashioned in homage to recording artist Post Malone, the headliner on the last night of the 2019 gathering.

**GLASSWARE: Collins glass**

**GARNISH: None**

- 1½ oz. Tito's Vodka
- ¼ oz. peach schnapps
- ¼ oz. Midori
- 2 oz. club soda, to top
- 2 oz. Sprite, to top

1. Add the vodka, schnapps, and Midori to a cocktail shaker filled with ice, shake vigorously until chilled, and strain into a Collins glass filled with ice.

2. Top with the club soda and Sprite.

## MIKE MOREY'S SIP 'N' TIP

Mike Morey was a local attorney, good neighbor, and a friend of the Downtown Cocktail Room (see page 266). He was the perennial great guest. He was friendly, generous, a great conversationalist and raconteur, but most importantly, he could drink all night and walk out on his own two feet. Morey's signature response when asked how he was doing, would be, "Just sippin' 'n' tippin'." He died suddenly in 2015, and on January 27, 2017, this place was named in his honor. It has been a big hit with locals ever since, whether they're looking for a good cocktail or to pay homage to a good friend.

# – THE MOREY –

in, vermouth, and bitters—an easy-peasy twist on the Martini.

**GLASSWARE:** Coupe

**GARNISH:** Orange twist

- **2 oz. Old Tom gin**
- **¾ oz. dry vermouth**
- **2 dashes orange bitters**

1. Add all of the ingredients to a mixing glass filled with ice, stir until chilled, and strain into the coupe.

2. Garnish with the orange twist

# – RHUBARB REFRESHER –

I f you can't track down the rhubarb bitters, substitute any sweet-and-tart bitters, such as grapefruit or cranberry.

- 1½ oz. London Dry gin
- 1 oz. Aperol
- 3 dashes rhubarb bitters
- ½ oz. fresh lime juice
- Ginger beer, to top

1. Add all of the ingredients, except for the ginger beer, to a cocktail shaker filled with ice, shake vigorously until chilled, and strain over ice into a rocks glass.

2. Top with the ginger beer and garnish with the lime wedge.

# – MELLOW HIGH –

The mint-spiked syrup is a fun touch to this cocktail, adding a robust flavor that must be experienced to be believed.

GLASSWARE: **Highball glass**

GARNISH: **Lemon wedge**

- 1½ oz. vodka
- ¾ oz. apricot liqueur or apricot brandy
- 1 oz. Mint Tea Syrup
- 1½ oz. fresh lemon juice

1. Add all of the ingredients to a cocktail shaker filled with ice, shake vigorously until chilled, and strain into a highball glass filled with ice.

2. Garnish with the lemon wedge.

MINT TEA SYRUP: Bring 2 cups of water to a boil in a saucepan and add 2 bags of peppermint tea. Reduce heat and simmer for 10 minutes. Remove the tea bags and add 2 cups sugar. Simmer, stirring the tea until the sugar has dissolved. Remove from heat and let cool completely before using or storing.

# OAK & IVY

Located in Container Park, so named for being built of nothing but old shipping containers, this eclectic spot is perfect for locals and visitors alike.

# – MULE SUGAR –

O ak & Ivy has an entire section of its menu dedicated to "Kickin' Mules." (Get it?) This one leans more traditional than some others, but it sure hits the spot.

- 1½ oz. Absolut Vodka
- 1½ oz. ginger beer
- 1½ oz. fresh lime juice
- 2 dashes aromatic bitters

1. Add the vodka and ginger beer to the copper mug and fill with ice.

2. Add the lime juice and bitters, stir gently until chilled, and garnish with a sprig of mint and a dusting of confectioners' sugar.

# – APPLE PIE HARVEST –

T here is a lot of sweet going on in this drink, hence the Becherovka, a Czech herbal bitter traditionally used as a digestive aid at the end of a meal. Garnish with caution.

**GLASSWARE: Rocks glass**

**GARNISH: Insta-Apple Pie and pipette of Becherovka**

- 1½ oz. Clyde May's Alabama Whiskey
- ¾ oz. fresh lemon juice
- ¾ oz. Simple Syrup (see page 15, use brown sugar)
- 3 dashes Bar Keep Apple Bitters
- ¾ oz. egg white

1. Add all of the ingredients to a cocktail shaker filled with ice, shake vigorously until chilled, and strain into a glass. Discard the ice, return the cocktail to the shaker, and dry shake for 15 seconds.

2. Strain over ice into a rocks glass and garnish with the Insta-Apple Pie and a pipette of Becherovka.

INSTA-APPLE PIE: Build this garnish on top of a slice of Granny Smith Apple, starting with a pad of unsalted butter. Follow with 2 teaspoons of brown sugar and 4 dashes of high-proof whiskey. Torch or broil the apple until crispy.

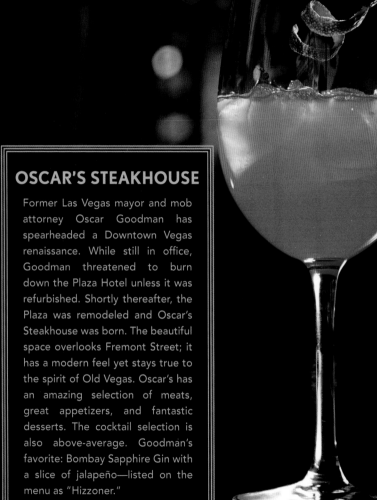

## OSCAR'S STEAKHOUSE

Former Las Vegas mayor and mob attorney Oscar Goodman has spearheaded a Downtown Vegas renaissance. While still in office, Goodman threatened to burn down the Plaza Hotel unless it was refurbished. Shortly thereafter, the Plaza was remodeled and Oscar's Steakhouse was born. The beautiful space overlooks Fremont Street; it has a modern feel yet stays true to the spirit of Old Vegas. Oscar's has an amazing selection of meats, great appetizers, and fantastic desserts. The cocktail selection is also above-average. Goodman's favorite: Bombay Sapphire Gin with a slice of jalapeño—listed on the menu as "Hizzoner."

# – RED LIGHT DISTRICT –

The flashy appearance and the complex experience awaiting you makes the Red Light District a perfect Vegas cocktail.

GLASSWARE: **Wine glass**

GARNISH: **Lime twist**

- **2 oz. vodka**
- **1 oz. Aperol**
- **½ oz. apricot liqueur**
- **½ oz. fresh lime juice**
- **½ oz. Simple Syrup (see page 15)**

1. Add all of the ingredients to a cocktail shaker filled with ice, shake vigorously until chilled, and strain over ice into a wine glass.

2. Garnish with the lime twist.

# – CONSIGLIERE –

Cherry Heering's intense flavor carries notes of marzipan, coriander, and sour cherries. It also has a syrupy texture. If you are a fan of all things cherry, this is the liqueur, and cocktail, for you.

GLASSWARE: **Snifter**

GARNISH: **None**

- 2½ oz. bourbon
- ½ oz. Cherry Heering
- ¾ oz. sweet vermouth

1. Add all of the ingredients to a mixing glass filled with ice, stir until chilled, and strain into the snifter.

The secret ingredient here is the aquafaba, which is the liquid that results from cooking beans (usually chickpeas). You don't have to soak dried beans and cook them to get it though, just crack open a can of chickpeas and use the liquid. It's gaining popularity as an vegan alternative to egg white.

GLASSWARE: **Rocks glass**

GARNISH: **Seasonal berries**

- **2 oz. Empress 1908 Indigo Gin**
- **¾ oz. fresh lemon juice**
- **¾ oz. aquafaba**
- **¾ oz. Simple Syrup (see page 15)**

1. Add all of the ingredients to a cocktail shaker filled with ice, shake vigorously until chilled, and strain over ice into a rocks glass.

2. Garnish with seasonal berries.

# A GOODMAN

As a lawyer, Oscar Goodman represented notorious figures like Meyer Lansky, Anthony Spilotro, and Frank Rosenthal. These names might sound familiar if you've seen the Martin Scorsese film *Casino*. Goodman even had a role in that film, appearing as himself and joking that he became mayor with the hope that it would position him to be in every movie that was shot in Las Vegas. It just so happens that a permit is needed in order to film any commercial, television show, or documentary in the city, and the mayor is the one to sign and approve production. Goodman is quite the jokester, but proved to be successful in getting himself in front of the camera once again when he was cast as himself in an episode of *CSI*.

When Goodman finished his terms, his wife, Carolyn Goodman, was elected mayor in 2011. She has continued to promote growth in Downtown Las Vegas, and played a key part in bringing professional sports to the valley.

## THE UNDERGROUND

The Mob Museum is a popular destination (see page 307), but the speakeasy that sits just beneath it has received just as much praise. Since speakeasy-styled bars have increased in Vegas over the years, it was only fitting for the Mob Museum to join the party. The Underground is filled with Prohibition Era artifacts and photos, as well as a well-stocked bar serving, you guessed it, Prohibition-inspired cocktails. To enter the side door, you will need the special password.

# – MOONSHINE MAYHEM –

**M**oonshine has gone mainstream in the last few decades, but there's still a delicious sense of mischief when it pops up.

GLASS: **Nick & Nora glass**
GARNISH: **Dehydrated pineapple wheel**

- **2 oz. Moonshine Infusion**
- **½ oz. pineapple juice**
- **¼ oz. Simple Syrup (see page 15, made with brown sugar)**

1. Add all of the ingredients to a cocktail shaker filled with ice, shake vigorously until chilled, and strain into the Nick & Nora glass.

2. Garnish with the dehydrated pineapple wheel.

MOONSHINE INFUSION: Peel and slice 1 pineapple. Place the pineapple pieces and a 750 ml bottle of 100-proof moonshine, 6 cardamom pods, and 2 lemon peels in a mason jar and let sit for 1 week. After 1 week, add 1 bag of Earl Grey tea and let steep for 2 hours, stirring occasionally. Remove the tea bag and lemon peels, puree the mixture in a blender, and double-strain before using or storing.

Blackberries, bourbon, and Sherry make for a velvety drink sure to please any flapper.

**GLASSWARE:** Rocks glass

**GARNISH:** Blackberry and sprig of fresh rosemary

- 3 blackberries
- 1½ oz. Maker's Mark bourbon whisky
- ¾ oz. cream Sherry
- ¼ oz. fresh lemon juice
- ½ oz. Rosemary Syrup (see page 121)
- 1 sprig of fresh rosemary

1. Add the blackberries to a cocktail shaker and muddle. Add ice and the remaining ingredients, shake vigorously until chilled, and double-strain over ice into the rocks glass.

2. Garnish with a blackberry and a sprig of rosemary.

# MOB MUSEUM

The Mob Museum, a nonprofit organization with a mission to advance the public understanding of organized crime's history and impact on American society, offers guests an interactive journey through the origins of organized crime in the US to its appearances in today's headlines. Awarded accreditation by the American Alliance of Museums, hands-on specialty exhibits and one-of-a-kind mob and law enforcement–related artifacts are all housed inside the restored courthouse and post office.

The museum's basement is home to The Underground speakeasy and a distillery exhibition, which centers around a working still that produces moonshine the way the mob did during Prohibition.

**THERAPY**

# — THE SMASH —

The Smash is one of Therapy's most popular cocktails. In fact, this cocktail is featured on the Lip Smacking Foodie Tour, a guided tour that spirits folks to some of the city's most historic spots and its buzzworthy new restaurants.

**GLASSWARE: Rocks glass**

**GARNISH: Sprig of fresh mint dusted with confectioners' sugar**

- **5 blackberries**
- **6 fresh mint leaves**
- **¾ oz. Simple Syrup (see page 15)**
- **¾ oz. fresh lime juice**
- **2 oz. Four Roses Bourbon**
- **Sprite, to top**

1. Add the blackberries, mint, syrup, and lime juice to a rocks glass and muddle.

2. Add ice and the bourbon, top up with the Sprite, and stir to combine.

3. Garnish with the sprig of mint dusted with confectioners' sugar.

VELVETEEN RABBIT

# – BLOOD OF MY ENEMIES –

Velveteen Rabbit is a community- and art-driven space that hosts singers, bands, comedians, and theater. Be inspired and transformed when you walk in, and don't be surprised if you smell incense, receive a tarot card reading, or drink a few herbal, smoky cocktails, in the vein of the Blood of My Enemies.

GLASSWARE: **Goblet**

GARNISH: **Fresh sage leaf**

- 1½ oz. Sage-Infused Rye
- ¾ oz. fresh lemon juice
- ½ oz. Simple Syrup (see page 15)
- 1 egg white
- ¼ oz. Frederiksdal Kirsebaervin Reserve wine, to float

1. Add all of the ingredients, except for the wine, to a cocktail shaker filled with ice, shake vigorously until chilled, and strain over ice into a goblet.

2. Float the wine on top of the cocktail and garnish with the sage leaf.

FOR SAGE-INFUSED RYE: Add 2 bunches of sage to a 750 bottle of rye whiskey and let steep for 24 to 48 hours. Strain before using or storing.

# – POP'S SECRET –

A fun drink to make at home. Not only does it involve popcorn, a crowd favorite, but the minty, coniferous notes of the Strega add a nice touch. The subtle hints of paprika in the popcorn and fennel bitters are a great combination, and not often associated with cocktails.

GLASSWARE: **Coupe**

GARNISH: **Paprika-seasoned popcorn**

- • **1 oz. Popcorn-Infused Mezcal**
- • **½ oz. Strega**
- • **¾ oz. fresh lemon juice**
- • **½ oz. Simple Syrup (see page 15)**
- • **1 dash fennel bitters**

1. Add all of the ingredients to a cocktail shaker filled with ice, shake vigorously until chilled, and strain over ice into a coupe.

2. Garnish with pieces of paprika-seasoned popcorn.

POPCORN-INFUSED MEZCAL: Add 2 cups buttered popcorn to a 750 ml bottle of mezcal and let steep for 24 hours. Strain before using or storing.

# WHERE TO EAT

These days, cocktails and cuisine go hand-in-hand. Foraged, seasonal, and local ingredients abound on both food and drink menus, which means you won't go hungry while sampling Vegas' cocktail culture. Here are a few spots that are a bit under the radar, but popular with locals and visitors alike, perfect to hit between drinks, or when you want something substantial in your stomach before calling it a night.

Grab a beer and a bite at the **TENAYA CREEK BREWERY** on West Bonanza Road, where a different food truck parks every day of the week. You'll find all the classic munchies, from pizza to Mexican food, burgers, and hot dogs.

**TACOS EL GORDO** is a must! This popular late-night stop on The Strip is famous for its Tijuana-inspired street food. Expect this place to be packed, and do not limit your order to just one taco.

If you have a sweet tooth, be sure to check out **LUV-IT FROZEN CUSTARD**. Opened in 1973, this frozen custard shop is a Vegas touchstone. The Scotch Jimmie Sundae is a go-to for butterscotch lovers, but if you're in the mood for something simple, just order the vanilla custard. Each month they feature a new flavor, so you can try everything if you're an adventurous sort!

Open 24 hours at the LINQ Hotel on The Strip (the other locations in the city close around 10:00 p.m.) **HASH HOUSE A GO GO** never disappoints, no matter which one you hit. Known for its fried chicken waffle tower, meatloaf, tractor-sized pancakes, and stuffed burgers, it's best to show up here hungry, because the portions are massive.

Located on Las Vegas Boulevard between the Wynn and the Riviera, **PEPPERMILL** does the classic, 24/7 diner Vegas-style, which means lots of neon, 64 oz. Scorpion cocktails, and slots.

**PARK ON FREMONT**, located in Downtown, has a laid-back outdoor dining area with a garden full of plants, flowers, and mismatched antique tables and chairs. Sneak around to the very back to find a seesaw that even some regulars do not know about. The elevated pub grub on the menu has something for everyone, and if you're visiting in the winter, enjoy a spiked coffee while cozied up next to the fire pit.

If you are into breakfast for dinner, head on over to the Mirage and check out the **THE PANTRY**, which never closes.

Those searching for a slice need to know about **SECRET PIZZA**: the only way to know about this New York-style slice joint is if someone gives you the inside scoop. Well, here's your inside scoop. Head on over to the third floor of the Cosmopolitan Hotel. There is no signage, just follow the unassuming hallway lined with record sleeves until you arrive in the promised land.

A few more:

**GÄBI COFFEE & BAKERY** is a speakeasy-style coffee shop, serving craft beverages and artisan pastries. A great place to quietly sip a latte while taking in the eclectic decor.

**CHICAGO JOE'S** is located on 4th Street in Downtown. Sitting in a quaint brick home, a trip to Vegas is not complete without visiting this Italian-American restaurant.

**MONTA RAMEN** is a hole-in-the-wall ramen joint on Spring Mountain Road. To avoid a long wait, make sure you go at off-hours.

For a Japanese-French dessert, wander off The Strip to **SWEETS RAKU**, take a seat at the bar, and watch immensely talented pastry chefs create tantalizing works of art. The perfect way to end date night with your special someone.

# INDEX

absinthe
  Circe's Kiss, 267
  F*ck the Pain Away, 237
  Lavender Lover, 268
accessories, 17
Acqua di Vida, 100
Adios Mother F'er (or AMF), 213
Alex & Piper, 207
All the Feels, 278
amaretto, Margarita Veneziana, 41
Amaro Averna, Let It Happen, 234
Amaro Meletti, Il Georgio, 148
Amaro Nonino, Barrel-Aged Old Fashioned, 23
Amaro Pasubio, I Plum Forgot, 165
Ancho Reyes, Jacqueline's Revenge, 171
Aperol
  Atomic Fizz, 135
  Brunch in Milan, 215
  Disgruntled Mai Tai, 63
  Hunter S. Mash, 254
  Il Georgio, 148
  Italian Highball, 99
  Milano, 95
  Nolet Us Pray, 147
  Owen's Spritz, 145
  Red Light District, 297
  Rhubarb Refresher, 288
  Sink the Pink, 233
Apple Pie Harvest, 294
apricot brandy, Mellow High, 291
apricot liqueur
  Mellow High, 291
  Red Light District, 297
Apricot Puree, 215
aquafaba
  Circe's Kiss, 267
  Paradiso, 152
  Q 1908, 300
Atomic Fizz, 135

Baileys Irish Cream, Cake Boss, 37
Banco de Mexico, 115
Barrel-Aged Old Fashioned, 23
Barrel-Aged Tony Negroni, 90
Basil Shrub, 253
Be Cool-ada, 265
Behold the Gold, 139
Bénédictine, Scotch 80s, 271
Berretto da Notte, 183
Bigallet China-China liqueur, The Kingsman, 274–275
Birds of Paradise, 195
Bitter Truth EXR Amaro, The Kingsman, 274–275
Blackberry Bourbon Lemonade, 155
Blackberry Puree
  Blackberry Bourbon Lemonade, 155
  recipe for, 155
  Rum 'n' Bramble, 132
Blood of My Enemies, 311
Blood Orange Sorbet, 183
Blue Mariner, 247
Blue Mariner Curaçao, 247
Blueberry Kombucha Mojito, 199
Bound Old Fashioned, 29
bourbon
  Barrel-Aged Old Fashioned, 23
  Blackberry Bourbon Lemonade, 155
  Bound Old Fashioned, 29
  Campfire S'mores, 229
  Consigliere, 298
  I Plum Forgot, 165
  Jacqueline's Revenge, 171
  The Marlow, 304
  The Maverick, 67
  The Midnight Rambler, 204
  Night at the Opera, 97
  The Smash, 309
  Southern Revival, 156
  Yardbird Old Fashioned, 159
Brachetto d'Acqui, I Plum

  Forgot, 165
brandy, Clarified Milk Punch, 175
Break the Rules, 220
Brunch in Milan, 215
Buol Mule, 124
Butterfly Bitter, 231

cachaca, Video Killed the Radio Star, 49
Caffe Lolita liqueur, Coconut White Russian, 61
Cake Boss, 37
Campari
  Barrel-Aged Tony Negroni, 90
  Strawberry Fields, 253
Campfire S'mores, 229
Casoni 1814 Aperitivo, All the Feels, 278
Catalunya, 185
cava, Catalunya, 185
Chambord, Raspberry Lemon Drop, 44
Chamomile Syrup, 267
Champagne, Thank You Very Matcha, 201
Charcoal Water, 82
Cherry Heering
  Consigliere, 298
  Mustache Ride, 27
Chive Dust, 241
chocolate liqueur
  Cake Boss, 37
  Milky Way Martini, 221
Cinnamon Sugar, 277
Cinnamon Syrup, 277
Circe's Kiss, 267
Clarified Milk Punch, 175
Coco Lopez Cream of Coconut, Scurvy, 193
Coconut Cream, 49, 61
Coconut Lychee Berry Liqueur, Mr. Coco, 107
Coconut White Russian, 61
Cointreau
  Demon Rhumba, 190
  Hibiscus Cosmo, 196

Paradiso, 152
  Scratch Margarita, 136
Consigliere, 298
Cosmo Mix, 68
Cosmopolitan Flight, 68
cream sherry, The Marlow,
  304
crème de cacao
  Banco de Mexico, 115
  Campfire S'mores, 229
  Espresso Martini, 43
crème de fleur, Pink Jasmine
  Martini, 142
crème de fruits de la passion,
  Video Killed the Radio
  Star, 49
crème de pêche, 67
crème de violette
  Lavender Lover, 268
  Monkey's Aviation, 224
Cucumber Stiletto, 128
Curaçao
  Acqua di Vida, 100
  Adios Mother F'er (or AMF),
  213
  Barrel-Aged Old Fashioned,
  23
  Blue Mariner, 247
  Cynar, Mole Negroni, 72

Dehydrated Peach Slice, 237
Demon Rhumba, 190
Destroyer, The, 78
Disgruntled Mai Tai, 63
Dolin Blanc, All the Feels, 278
Dolin Genepy le Chamois,
  Saru 47, 117
Domaine de Canton
  Behold the Gold, 139
  Il Georgio, 148
  The Rested Root, 30
  The Vicky, 108
Don't Cry Wolf, 240–241
Dope Hat, 81
Drago Roso, 38

Edo Gin & Tonic, 186
Elderflower Syrup, 33
Elephant in the Room, 239
Elizabeth's Gin & Tonic, 203
Espresso Martini, 43

F. W. Margarita, 54
F*ck the Pain Away, 237
Fat Cap, 86
Flaming Lime Shell, 247
Flor de la Piña, 57
Foie Gras-Washed High West
  Double Rye, 243
Frederiksdal Kirsebaervin
  Reserve wine, Blood of My
  Enemies, 311
Fresno Chili Syrup, 54
Frosted Berries, 103

G, 77
Gatsby's Gin Fiz, 24
Get Him to the Greek, 59
gin
  Adios Mother F'er (or AMF),
  213
  Barrel-Aged Tony Negroni,
  90
  Circe's Kiss, 267
  Clarified Milk Punch, 175
  Edo Gin & Tonic, 186
  Elephant in the Room, 239
  Elizabeth's Gin & Tonic, 203
  Gatsby's Gin Fiz, 24
  Get Him to the Greek, 59
  Infused Sipsmith Gin, 186
  Lavender Lover, 268
  Lavender-Infused Gin, 268
  Level 55: Ghostbar, 125
  Limey Son of a Gun, 169
  London Commons, 258
  Monkey's Aviation, 224
  The Morey, 287
  Negroni Bianco, 112
  Nolet Us Pray, 147
  Pink Jasmine Martini, 142
  Pretty in Pink, 166
  Q 1908, 300
  Rhubarb Refresher, 288
  Rook, 82
  Saru 47, 117
  Sink the Pink, 233
  Strawberry Fields, 253
  Thank You Very Matcha, 201
  Unicorns & Sunshine, 219
ginger beer
  Buol Mule, 124
  F*ck the Pain Away, 237
  Mule Sugar, 293
  Owen's Mega Mule, 141
  Rhubarb Refresher, 288
ginger liqueur, The Rested
  Root, 30
Ginger Syrup
  Hunter S. Mash, 254
  recipe for, 50
  Verbena, 50
Gourmet Lemon, 245
Grenadine, Homemade, 100
Guinness Draught, Mustache
  Ride, 27

Hennessy VSOP, Sidecar, 172
Hibiscus & Habanero Syrup
  Flor de la Piña, 57
  Mezcal Sun, 71
  recipe for, 57
Hibiscus Cosmo, 196
Hibiscus Syrup, 196
home-bar setup, 13–17
Honey Syrup
  Catalunya, 185
  recipe for, 185
  Saru 47, 117
Hunter S. Mash, 254

I Plum Forgot, 165
Il Georgio, 148
Infused Sipsmith Gin, 186
Insta-Apple Pie, 294
Italian Highball, 99
Italicus Rosolio di Bergamotto
  Level 55: Ghostbar, 125
  Negroni Bianco, 112
  Video Killed the Radio Star,
  49

Jacqueline's Revenge, 171
Jalapeño-Infused Jameson
  Irish Whiskey, 81
Jardín Fresco, 181

Kahlùa
  Espresso Martini, 43
  Spark Plug, 223
Kingsman, The, 274–275

Las Vegas, about, 7–11
Lavender Lover, 268
Lavender-Infused Gin,
  Lavender Lover, 268
Let It Happen, 234
Level 55: Ghostbar, 125
Limey Son of a Gun, 169
limoncello
  Gourmet Lemon, 245
  VGK Puck Drop, 227
liqueurs for home bar, 15
Little Hot Mess, 257
London Commons, 258
Luxardo Amaretto-Angostura
  Bitters House Mix, 107
Luxardo Bitter Bianco,
  Negroni Bianco, 112

Mac 'n' Slosh, 277
Malibu, Pineapple Under the
  Sea, 179
Mango Martini, 217
maraschino cherry liqueur,
  Monkey's Aviation, 224
Margarita Veneziana, 41
Marie Brizard Royal Chocolat,
  Cake Boss, 37
Marlow, The, 304
Matcha Agave, 201
Maverick, The, 67
Mellow High, 291
Meringue, 245
mezcal
  Banco de Mexico, 115
  Don't Cry Wolf, 240–241
  Mezcal Sun, 71
  Mole Negroni, 72
  Old Smokey Knights, 118
  Popcorn-Infused Mezcal,
  312
  Pop's Secret, 312
  Thai Chili Mezcal, 241
Midnight Rambler, The, 204
Midori
  Northern Lights, 104

Post Melon, 284
Milano, 95
Milky Way Martini, 221
Mint Tea Syrup, 291
mixers, 15–16
Mole Negroni, 72
Monkey's Aviation, 224
Moonshine Infusion, 303
Moonshine Mayhem, 303
Morey, The, 287
Mr. Coco, 107
Mule Sugar, 293
Mustache Ride, 27

Negroni Bianco, 112
Night at the Opera, 97
Nolet Us Pray, 147
Northern Lights, 104

Old Smokey Knights, 118
orange liqueur, Sidecar, 172
Orgeat, 63
Owen's Mega Mule, 141
Owen's Spritz, 145

Paddington, 261
Pallini Limoncello, The Vicky, 108
Papaya Jam, 53
Paradiso, 152
passion fruit wine, Butterfly Bitter, 231
Patron Citronge Mango, Paradiso, 152
peach schnapps
  Birds of Paradise, 195
  Frosted Berries, 103
  Post Melon, 284
pear liqueur
  F*ck the Pain Away, 237
  Utopia, 123
Pepperoni Pizza Bloody Mary, 283
Pesto Syrup, 82
Pineapple Under the Sea, 179
Pink Jasmine Martini, 142
pisco, G, 77
Plum Flower, 165
Plum Syrup, 165
pomegranate liqueur, Drago Roso, 38
Pomegranate Syrup, 195
Popcorn-Infused Mezcal, 312
Pop's Secret, 312
Post Melon, 284
Pretty in Pink, 166
Prosecco
  All the Feels, 278
  Berretto da Notte, 183
  Brunch in Milan, 215
  Jardín Fresco, 181
  Milano, 95

Q 1908, 300
Queen's Park Swizzle, 89

Rabarbaro Zucca, Mole Negroni, 72
Rapa Giovanni Amaro, Let It Happen, 234
Raspberry Lemon Drop, 44
Reàl Cream of Coconut, Be Cool-ada, 265
Red Light District, 297
Rested Root, The, 30
Rhubarb Refresher, 288
Rhubarb Syrup, 278
Roasted Grapefruit Wheel, 166
Roasted Pineapple Juice, 86
Rook, 82
Rosemary Syrup
  recipe for, 121
  The Marlow, 304
  The Maverick, 67
  Walk This Way, 121
rum
  Acqua di Vida, 100
  Adios Mother F'er (or AMF), 213
  Be Cool-ada, 265
  Birds of Paradise, 195
  Blue Mariner, 247
  Blueberry Kombucha Mojito, 199
  Catalunya, 185
  Demon Rhumba, 190
  Disgruntled Mai Tai, 63
  Little Hot Mess, 257
  Mac 'n' Slosh, 277
  Mr. Coco, 107
  Northern Lights, 104
  Queen's Park Swizzle, 89
  Rum 'n' Bramble, 132
  Scurvy, 193
  Tonga Reefer, 189
rye
  Blood of My Enemies, 311
  The Kingsman, 274–275
  Paddington, 261
  Rye Candy-and-Chocolate Covered Bacon, 274–275
  Sage-Infused Rye, 311
  Scrooge McDuck, 242

Sage-Infused Rye, 311
Salers Gentiane Aperitif, Limey Son of a Gun, 169
Saru 47, 117
Scotch
  Black Islay Mustache, 27
  Buol Mule, 124
  Scotch 80s, 271
Scotch 80s, 271
Scratch Margarita, 136
Scrooge McDuck, 242
Scurvy, 193
sherry
  Night at the Opera, 97
  The Vicky, 108
Sichuan Foam, 241

Sidecar, 172
Sink the Pink, 233
Smash, The, 309
soju, Butterfly Bitter, 231
Some Like It Hot, 53
Something Delicious, 47
Sour Mix
  Recipe for, 177
  Strip Tini, 177
  Vegas Heart, 211
VGK Puck Drop, 227
Southern Revival, 156
Spark Plug, 223
Spice of Love, 131
Spiced Coconut Foam, 49
Spiced Honey Syrup, 49
Spicy Fifty, 33
Spiked Lemonade, 209
spirits for home bar, 14–15
St-Germain
  Berretto da Notte, 183
  Cucumber Stiletto, 128
  Jardín Fresco, 181
  Something Delicious, 47
  Strawberry Fields, 253
  Strip Tini, 177
Stiegl Beagle, 263
Stiegl Radler Grapefruit, Stiegl Beagle, 263
stout, Campfire S'mores, 229
Strawberry Cobbler, 127
Strawberry Fields, 253
Strawberry-Infused Tequila, 278
Strega, Pop's Secret, 312
Strip Tini, 177
Sweet & Sour
  Adios Mother F'er (or AMF), 213
  Demon Rhumba, 190
  recipe for, 190
  Scurvy, 193

Tattooed Orange Peel, 234
techniques and terms, 16–17
tequila
  Adios Mother F'er (or AMF), 213
  Alex & Piper, 207
  All the Feels, 278
  Banco de Mexico, 115
  Behold the Gold, 139
  The Destroyer, 78
  Don't Cry Wolf, 240–241
  F. W. Margarita, 54
  Fat Cap, 86
  Flor de la Piña, 57
  Gourmet Lemon, 245
  Il Georgio, 148
  Jardín Fresco, 181
  Let It Happen, 234
  Margarita Veneziana, 41
  Mezcal Sun, 71
  Old Smokey Knights, 118
  The Rested Root, 30

Scratch Margarita, 136
Some Like It Hot, 53
Stiegl Beagle, 263
Strawberry-Infused Tequila, 278
Vegas Heart, 211
Verbena, 50
Thai Chili Mezcal, 241
Thank You Very Matcha, 201
Tonga Reefer, 189
tools, 13–14
triple sec
    Mango Martini, 217
    Paddington, 261
    Raspberry Lemon Drop, 44
    Something Delicious, 47

Unicorns & Sunshine, 219
Utopia, 123

Vanilla Syrup, 123
Vegas Heart, 211
velvet falernum, The Rested Root, 30
Verbena, 50
VGK Puck Drop, 227
Vicky, The, 108
Video Killed the Radio Star, 49

vodka
    Adios Mother F'er (or AMF), 213
    Atomic Fizz, 135
    Brunch in Milan, 215
    Cake Boss, 37
    Coconut White Russian, 61
    Cosmopolitan Flight, 68
    Cucumber Stiletto, 128
    Drago Roso, 38
    Espresso Martini, 43
    F*ck the Pain Away, 237
    Frosted Berries, 103
    Hibiscus Cosmo, 196
    Italian Highball, 99
    Mango Martini, 217
    Mellow High, 291
    Milano, 95
    Milky Way Martini, 221
    Mr. Coco, 107
    Mule Sugar, 293
    Owen's Mega Mule, 141
    Owen's Spritz, 145
    Paradiso, 152
    Pepperoni Pizza Bloody Mary, 283
    Pineapple Under the Sea, 179

Post Melon, 284
Raspberry Lemon Drop, 44
Red Light District, 297
Saru 47, 117
Something Delicious, 47
Spark Plug, 223
Spice of Love, 131
Spicy Fifty, 33
Spiked Lemonade, 209
Strawberry Cobbler, 127
Strip Tini, 177
VGK Puck Drop, 227
The Vicky, 108

Walk This Way, 121
whiskey
    Apple Pie Harvest, 294
    Break the Rules, 220
    Dope Hat, 81
    Hunter S. Mash, 254
    Jalapeño-Infused Jameson Irish Whiskey, 81
    Mustache Ride, 27
    Scotch 80s, 271
    Utopia, 123
    Walk This Way, 121

Yardbird Old Fashioned, 159

# ABOUT THE AUTHOR

Sivan Gavish is the creator of the blog, The Olive Brunette, which is dedicated to providing an inside look into Las Vegas. Her passion for her hometown does not go unnoticed and she has made it her mission to give others the ultimate tour of this internationally renowned city. In addition to writing, she enjoys photography and editing, as well as attending shows and events on The Strip. Gavish holds a BA in Journalism and Media Studies from the University of Nevada, Las Vegas. And she has a black belt in Tae Kwon Do!

—ABOUT CIDER MILL PRESS BOOK PUBLISHERS—

Good ideas ripen with time. From seed to harvest, Cider Mill Press
brings fine reading, information, and entertainment together between
the covers of its creatively crafted books. Our Cider Mill bears fruit
twice a year, publishing a new crop of titles each spring and fall.

CIDER MILL
PRESS

BOOK
PUBLISHERS
KENNEBUNKPORT, MAINE

"Where Good Books Are Ready for Press"

Visit us on the web at
cidermillpress.com

or write to us at
PO Box 454
12 Spring St.
Kennebunkport, Maine 04046